MAP OF
CALIFORNIA

GENERAL AREA
OCCUPIED BY
THE WINTU
(After Kroeber)

f Bones

The Wintu Myths of a Trinity River Indian

by

Marcelle Masson

NATUREGRAPH PRESS

Preface by Dr. Adan E. Treganza

Illustrations by Charles E. Masson, Jr.

NATUREGRAPH COMPANY

Library of Congress Card Number 66-23398

SBN (paper) 911010-26-2
SBN (cloth) 911010-27-0

Acknowledgement

My thanks go to Dr. Adan E. Treganza for the encouragement he gave me in having the legends of our friend Grant Towendolly published, and for the preface he has supplied, and to Theodora Kroeber for her interest in the stories and her suggestions as to the arrangement of the material.

My appreciation is expressed to my daughter Valerie, my son Charles, and to Mr. Thomas F. Holler for their assistance in preparing the copy for publication.

Marcelle Masson

5558 Taft Avenue
Oakland, California 94618

Preface

The stories you are about to read represent one of
those rare but fortunate historical accidents where
the lives of several people have crossed and the result
of this contact, as brief as life is, has left a real con-
tribution to knowledge about a group of human beings
who in themselves are almost mythological - they are
the shattered remnants of the California Indians.

Not all California Indians were alike, for from north
to south and from east to west they varied greatly in
the language they spoke, the use of their natural land-
scape, their social and religious beliefs and, not to
be overlooked, their mythological records - call them
folk tales or simply "just so" stories, if you wish.
Such stories are important, for among those people
of the world who have been non-literate, the folk
stories told over and over embody the history and
insure the continuity of that group of people. With
no writing, oral tradition told over and over again
is what provides direction and behavioral guidance
to the social group. In these myths are to be found
aspects of Indian cosmogony, or in other words the
Indian's view of not only the universe but his relation
to it. Often his views are different from ours even
to the point where he attains the supreme intimacy of
participating in his total world instead of fighting it.
If the stories are read with care they will first bring
pleasure and with more examination there will emerge
value systems, patterns of thinking, kinship systems,
philosophies of life and adjustment, etc. Truly, stories of this sort can be exciting. It must be remember-
ed by the reader that the world view of many aboriginal

people differs in both degree and kind - yet it is humanistic. It is not more or less intelligent. Just different. The California Indians are no exception, for they, like many hunting and gathering folk, lived not only close to but were dependent upon nature for their survival. Indeed they were a part of nature and that's exactly how they felt about it. The human, plant and animal world constituted one area of interaction, most of the time harmonious but at times, like ours, conflicting. If necessary, "unworldly" or "outer worldly" creatures could be created to fill unexplained gaps in human understanding and knowledge. If one has doubts imagine what an Indian would think if he were unprepared and you told him of the "Easter Bunny" and his egg laying habit, Santa Claus and his bag of toys and his reindeer. And what of Halloween with its witches and goblins? We don't believe in such stories, we just perpetually keep telling and acting them out as part of our national and commercial heritage. Indians believed their stories from birth to death. Their story telling and ceremonies were to them what our libraries are to us - the total pool of knowledge. Where Santa Claus might fail, Genesis could be sold to an Indian, just as was the earlier story from the Gilgamish stone sold to the ancient Mesopotamians. All peoples have to explain how the world was created for man, though often aboriginal people think of creation and man and not for man. Noah must have communicated with candidates for the Ark; perfection must have been a basic qualification. But Noah must have had further powers of communication for he spread among their ears a taboo called a "thou shalt not." They embarked two-by-two and the same number had to disembark. Now really, our stories aren't so new and unique, are they!

To prepare you, if I haven't already, the peoples in these stories interacted with nature and they gave to the animal and bird world the ability to think, speak and respond like human beings. This way man and the biological world could communicate, but above this all the characters which occur in myth were endowed with super-human power.

PREFACE

The contributors to these stories are the Wintu Indians of the northern Sacramento Valley of California. They have been here all their lives, measured only in 1000's of years. The outsiders who took the time and interest to record these stories were Mr. and Mrs. Charles Masson. Especially Mrs. Masson is to be congratulated for bringing this work to its final conclusion.

The real character and creator of these stories is Laktcharas Tauhindauli, better known as Grant Towendolly, Wintu Indian, philosopher, mystic, shaman, and above all an intense human being who believed in life and man.

My contact with Grant was sporadic and for short periods of time, but the exchange between two people was open, warm and fluent. Grant lived in three worlds: the contemporary Caucasian world from which he had no escape; his Indian world which directed his inner feelings and emotions; and last, a world of the super-natural, for he was one of the last of the Wintu shamans. I am indebted to Mrs. Masson for introducing me to Towendolly for it was he who gave me the key to the ceremonial use of Samwell Cave and explained many of the heretofore mysteries surrounding it. The way Grant talked is the way Mrs. Masson recorded his stories and this is the way it should be. The way one talks is the way one thinks and the purpose of this book is to reveal how other people view the world. I have encouraged her to maintain this level and not turn it into a "Mother Goose" series. She has done a fine job. I hope the reader enjoys it. It is refreshing.

Adan E. Treganza
Professor of Anthropology
San Francisco State College

Table of Contents

CONTENTS

The author's illustrator-son, Charles, hoping to hear the deer
bones rattle in the Bag of Bones.

1 Introduction

By the side of an old Indian trail on Salt Creek in Shasta County, California, is a large balanced rock which the Indians of long ago called a "bag of bones." Deer bones could be heard rattling around inside, they said. My husband and I were told this by an Indian who should know: Grant Towendolly, a son of William Towendolly, former headman of a Trinity County group of the Wintu Indians.

Grant had been trained by his father for leadership, a preparation which included learning the myths and legends of his people and, an important point, the correct way to narrate these stories. For they must be told in a certain ceremonial way, with nothing omitted to simplify or abbreviate the narrative.

Here, then, are Grant's Wintu myths. More or less similar versions of several of these stories have appeared in collections of Indian myths made by anthropology students and by interested laymen. But what adds special interest to Grant's tales, I believe, is the fact that the reader is presented here with stories actually written by the Indian himself and, in this case, by an Indian who had been especially entrusted with the preservation of the authentic Trinity Wintu legends. Some of these stories, to my knowledge, have never before appeared in anthologies of Indian myths.

I have left intact the title, syntax and the composition of each legend as Grant wrote it in his untutored and inimitable English. Corrections have been made in

1

spelling and punctuation only when it seemed necessary for clarity.

The last five stories, however, beginning with "Sedit
and Kobalis," are some that Grant in his younger days
dictated to my husband's mother, the late Elda A.
Masson.

Grant's father died when he was too young to take his
father's place as the headman of the group, so an uncle,
who was known as "Chief Alexander," became the
interim leader. By the time Grant came of age the Wintu
were so dispersed by the advent of the white man that
tribal unity was lost and Grant never functioned as a
Wintu headman.

Fearing that what he considered to be the true Trinity
legends would die with him, Grant began to write down
some of the legends of his forefathers for us. Because
of the fact that my husband and Grant had been close
friends since boyhood we were especially privileged
to be on fairly intimate terms with him and thus were
honored by his confidence. We heard many of the
stories of his people and of his homeland from his
lips.

As background material I have preceded the Wintu myths
with a biographical sketch of the Towendolly family
which explains Grant's connection with the McCloud
and Masson families of Upper Soda Springs and elabo-
rates on his relation with my late husband, Charles E.
(Pete) Masson of Dunsmuir, California.

Considerable research has been done by anthropologists
on the various Northern California Indian groups and
subgroups, and anthropological journals are readily
available which describe the Indian's home and domestic
arrangements, his hunting and fishing techniques, his
activities as a gatherer of the plants, berries and acorns
which supplemented his diet, and the preparation of
these for consumption, and, further, his crafts, among
which basket weaving was prominent.

Because these data are available from many sources
and because my notes do not presume to the status of

a scientific treatise, I have, in the main, limited the chapter on the Indian's way of life to subjects we actually heard Grant discuss; for example, salmon fishing and the preparation of salmon for eating, the construction of a salmon spear pole, the processing of acorns for food, etc.

Lastly, I have included a chapter concocted from notes taken when my husband and I were out on hiking trips or longer jaunts by automobile with Grant. Streams, rocks, trees, canyons, cliffs and mountain peaks -- ordinary mountain scenery to our eyes -- so often held special significance for our Wintu companion and drew from him pertinent comments as to their peculiar role in Wintu legends, that it became wise for me to go prepared with notebook and pencil when a trip with Grant was planned.

As for the "bag of bones" on Salt Creek, Grant had promised us he would write the story of how the bones got there but he never did, and he is gone now. But my "bag of notes" has been figuratively "rattling around" in a desk drawer for a number of years asking for attention just as it seems the deer bones did (and assuredly still do) in the balanced rock on Salt Creek. My hope is that the reader may enjoy following the by-paths of the old Trinity Wintu Indians, that perhaps he may be inspired to look for the cave where the giants lived, or visit the Lake of the Bleeding Heart, or explore the homeland of Norwanchakas and Keriha and the other mythical people who lived in Trinity, Siskiyou and Shasta counties ages ago.

Even more interesting would it be to find a sandhill crane and look him in the face to see if he really is cross-eyed, as it is claimed in one of the stories of Sedit and Torraharsh.

Upper Soda Springs in the 1860's

2　The Towendolly Family

The tribal home of the Towendollys was at Hay Gulch in Trinity County. The father, Old Bill, as he was called by the white man, was a headman in his own right, his father before him having held that position. Their Indian family name was Tau-hin-dauli, which means "tying with the left hand." Grant's Wintu name was Laktcharas Tauhindauli.

Old Bill was married twice. His second wife was Jennie Stump, who was Grant's mother. She was from the Achomawi tribe of the Pit River Indians.

With the arrival of the white man in the area, the Towendollys left their ancestral home in Trinity County and settled on the Sacramento River at a place which became known as the Soda Springs and later, Upper Soda Springs (Mem-okis-takki: strong water place) in Siskiyou County (now within the city limits of Dunsmuir). They returned to Trinity County only for dances or occasional gatherings and were living on the Sacramento riverbank in Siskiyou when, in 1855, my husband's grandparents, Ross and Mary McCloud, bought the property from two squatters, Harry and Samuel Lockhart, twin brothers who became well known in the early day history of Shasta County.

Old Bill remained on the place to work for the McClouds. His opinion of some of the miners and settlers who were now taking over the home of his forefathers was neatly expressed when he once said to Mr. McCloud, "White man all time drink whisket, swear damn!"

The McClouds operated an inn at the place for the early-day travelers, using the log cabin that the Lockharts had built and then adding a larger two-story building of logs and shakes. In time members of the family had buildings of planed lumber constructed to take the place of the first crude hostelries and Soda Springs became a popular summer resort.

Grant, who was born at Upper Soda Springs on October 29, 1873, spent more than half his life there, working as a handyman and gardener, and growing up with my husband Charles (Pete) and his brothers Jim and Dick, grandsons of the McClouds and sons of John and Elda McCloud Masson who operated the resort until the early 1920s when it was permanently closed.

Grant had been chosen by his father to become the next chieftain* of the northern Wintu because he recognized in this son more than in his other sons the qualities that would be needed to withstand the rigorous training which was necessary. He stressed that he must always live right and that hell was on earth. There were periods of fasting, of being alone in the mountains; there was the learning to recognize the medicinal plants and to understand their use. Most important was knowing the myths and legends of his people and being able to tell

---

*According to ethnologists, the term "chief" used in a political sense, does not apply to all the California Indian tribes; instead, for some, it is used only in the sense of being the chief man or leader of the tribe or group. Cf. A. L. Kroeber, Elements of Culture in Native California (U. of Calif. Publications in American Archaeology and Ethnology, Berkeley, Calif., November, 1922), XIII, No. 8, 285-286: "Chieftainship is still wrapped up in much the same obscurity and vagueness as political bodies. There were no doubt hereditary chiefs in many parts of California....In general it seems that chieftainship was more definitely hereditary in the southern half or two thirds of the state than in the north central area. Wealth was a factor of some consequence in relation to chieftainship everywhere, but its influence seems also to have varied according to locality. The northwestern tribes had hereditarily rich men of great influence but no chiefs. Being without political organization, they could not well have had the latter."

them correctly.

Many whites now had settled in the Indians' homeland, and the bonds of tribal unity were weakened by dispersion and by intermarriage with the white man. A chieftain's duties became a thing of the past. The last "big gathering" of the Trinity Wintu, Grant said, was held in 1882. Their way of life began to change and, much to Grant's disgust, English began to adulterate the Wintu tongue.

In his youth Grant attended for a time an elementary school in the Bay area. He was sent there by Henry E. Highton, a prominent San Francisco lawyer who spent many summers in early days at Upper Soda Springs and who became very fond of Grant's father whom he always had as a guide on his hikes in the mountains.

Although Grant received this start on a white man's education and became an avid reader, he had no inclination towards becoming less Indian. He and his wife, Lillie Hunt Towendolly, a Pit River Indian, always spoke together in the Wintu tongue. Lillie continued to make baskets and to have an occasional bowl of acorn soup in season, albeit the concoction was cooked on her wood stove and not by the hot rock method of her ancestors.

When the Upper Soda Springs resort closed, Grant and Lillie had moved to an Indian allotment near O'Brien, in the hill country north of Redding in Shasta County. Grant's "rancheria," as he called it, had a small vegetable garden, chickens and four or five vociferous dogs. His two room home was neat but sparsely furnished. One summer we had an extra refrigerator which we thought Grant and Lillie could use, since, as he became older, he made fewer shopping trips and consequently found it more convenient to buy larger amounts of food each trip. We took our second-hand refrigerator down to him, thinking it would help solve his storage problem and keep his meat fresh. But something went wrong with the motor and Grant, who had always been able to repair anything, was unable to make it work properly. He became so exasperated with the obstinate machine that he took it out, hacked it to pieces,

carried the junk up into the hills and buried it, each
piece in a different place -- Grant's personal revolt
against the complexity of the mechanized twentieth
century.

Grant was a gentleman and a fine friend. He was the
last of his people, to our knowledge, who remained
true to the teachings of his ancestors and, more re-
markable in a white man's world, carried on the cus-
toms and rituals of the ancient Wintu leaders whenever possible. Grant was very proud of his lineage
and at one time said, "I am of royal blood as much
as the kings and queens of Europe are!"

He died on March 19, 1963 at the age of ninety. Lillie
preceded him in death by several years. At her funeral
service, conducted in the orthodox manner of today by
a minister who was part Indian, I was pleased to see
Grant, at the close of the service, give his nephew
a paper bag from which he took out many, many strings
of beads which he placed in Lillie's hands, in accord-
ance with an ancestral custom.

3   The Indians' Way of Life

The homes of the ancestors of our Indian friends were made to suit the area in which they happened to be located. In the mountains shacks of oak posts covered with cedar bark and branches served them very well. For something warmer, or for a more permanent dwelling, there was the earth lodge: a place in the ground scooped out, the dirt piled up around the edge and the roof made of poles and covered with branches and bark and more dirt. The sweat house was made of willows and opened to the south.

Fire was made by twirling a stick of the buckeye tree between the palms of the hands with the point of the stick placed on dry fir or cedar bark. Dry leaves were placed on it also, and the resulting sparks would turn into flames.

For roasting salmon, a hot fire was made in the center of a bed of small, flat rocks which had been placed in an area the size of a large table top, or larger. The ashes were pushed aside and the salmon, cleaned and with heads and tails cut off, were placed side by side on the hot rocks, opened side down. Large saxifrage leaves from the river bank were placed over the salmon, then the hot ashes. Slabs of fir bark were placed in readiness near by and the salmon, when sufficiently roasted, were taken out after first scraping aside the hot ashes and saxifrage, and were put on the smooth inner side of the bark and broken in pieces to hasten the cooling. When cool and dry enough for handling, the salmon pieces were worked by the fingers until pulverized as fine as meal. Sometimes salt was mixed

9

with the salmon flour and it would then keep until the
next summer, if necessary. The Indian in those far
off days obtained his salt from the beds occurring in
the area. Grant took us to one such place a few miles
northeast of Redding.

To smoke salmon it was split as before and a stick
placed near the top horizontally to keep the sides spread
open. Hung along a pole over a fire until dried, the
flat slabs of fish were then piled up in baskets until
needed. Meat and game were roasted on beds of hot
charcoal.

For variety in eating the meal the Indians would sometimes put in dried salmon eggs or sugarpine nuts.

Preparing acorns for their meals was a considerable
task for the Indian woman. The acorn shells were crack-
ed either with one's teeth or by rolling the acorn between two stones held in the hands. The cleaned a-
corn nuts were then put in a bottomless basket that
was placed on a flat rock and pounded with a stone
pestle until the nuts were pulverized as fine as flour.
The flour was then sifted through an open-work basket
("kh-nee") and piled up on clean, coarse, wet sand
that had been patted down in a depressed circle on the
ground. The flour was now leached by pouring first
cold water over it, then warm, until the bitterness was
gone. This chore consumed almost an entire day, Lillie
said.

When it tasted right, the uppermost part of the flour
was taken off and dried and then stored in baskets; the
flour next to the sand was put into another basket with
some water and stirred. It was left for the sand to
settle and, when ready, the broth was poured off into
another basket. It could then be heated for mealtime
by dropping into the basket several hot, clean and
smooth river rocks about the size of a grapefruit, or
larger.

When making acorn bread the flour was put on a hot,
flat rock and stirred with an oaken paddle called a
"to-loi-e." The flour had a natural oil in it and when
cooked it was taken off and flattened, or shaped into

a loaf for use.

The old-time Indian had a wide choice of vegetables
to include in his daily menu. One of importance was
the wild potato, which Grant called "tshet-in." This
tuber, about the length of a man's thumb, thick at the
base and tapering, is found in swampy places and has
tall leaves, according to Grant. The potatoes were
boiled by the hot rock method and often wild onions
were cooked with them.

The bulb of the brodiaea was also eaten, as well as
wild cabbage and clover. Young shoots of the saxifrage were pulled up in the springtime and eaten raw
by the Indians. Then there were wild raspberries,
blackberries and manzanita berries, used either fresh
or dried. From the latter a sweet brew was made.
Taking the dried tail of a deer, an Indian would sometimes dip it in the sweet brew, or manzanita cider,
and slowly pull it through his teeth, his version of
the white man's lollipop.

Mother Nature, in providing for her children, gave
them a tobacco plant also. Everything they needed
was there to be discovered by them. Sunflower roots
when burned served as a disinfectant -- and a hand-
ful of wild sage carried along on a deer hunt brought
good luck!

When making arrowheads the Indian tried to find a
small piece of flint closely resembling the required
shape. With a piece of deer hide in one palm to protect it, the hunter would place the flint in his palm,
rest his hand on his knee and then chip off the edges
of the obsidian with a deer horn until he had the finished
product.

Grizzly bear were shot with red flint, the Indian thinking it more deadly. This flint was found near Buckeye
in Shasta County.

Bows were made from the ash tree. The bow was
strengthened by glueing deer sinew along the outside,
the glue having been obtained by boiling down salmon
skin. The wild currant saplings were used to make the

arrows for killing birds. Tail feathers of the yellow-
hammer were used on the arrows.

A fishline could be made from a thread that was pulled
down or stripped from the two edges of the grass-like
leaves of a plant they called "poo-te-re." It is of the
wild iris family. By overlapping the threads and then
rolling them together on one's knee with the palm until
the desired length is reached, a fishline is produced
which can withstand any amount of pulling. The several
thicknesses give added strength.

A two-strand twist of the bark of the milkweed was also
used to make string. Another serviceable plant was
dogbane, with its fibrous bark.

A certain bone in the jaw of a deer made an excellent
fishhook. Serving the same purpose was a bone from
the jaw of what Grant called riffle pike.

Poles to spear salmon were about 15 feet long and were
made of fir. Pitch and ashes were put on the poles to
darken them. At the "business end" were fastened two
prongs about six or eight inches long, or longer, made
of wood from the serviceberry shrub, the ends of the
prongs wrapped securely to the pole with sinew. A
strip of deer sinew was tied midway of the prongs to
keep them from spreading and to give added strength
when spearing the fish.

A thimble made of a special kind of wood, or of a deer
bone, sharply pointed at one end, was placed on each
prong. Midway on these tips was tied a long, strong
cord of buckskin or line, the ends of which, with plenty
of slack, were tied to the spear pole. When the prongs
went through the fish the tips came off as the prongs
were withdrawn, thus leaving the salmon hanging to the
spear pole by the toggles. Grant said the Indians
wrapped grass around the toggles when pulling them
out.

When salmon were spawning there would always be a
big male below the spawning bed, chasing the trout
away; the Indians knew this was the best place to fish
for trout, just below the spawning bed.

My husband said that Johnny, an older half-brother of Grant, used to go to a certain gravel bar in the river at Upper Soda Springs where the salmon always spawned. He'd get so many trout there at the time of spawning that he'd have to stop because his hands got so slippery from the fish.

In spearing the salmon Johnny would put his spear in the water ahead of the salmon and let it float down as he held it, and when it got opposite the salmon he'd jab it, never missing. He seemed to understand what the refraction of light could do and took that into consideration, realizing that the salmon was actually deeper in the water than it appeared to be. To my husband, as a young lad watching him, it seemed that the spear was much too high in the water and would go above the salmon. This same deceptive illusion is what made it necessary to seem to aim underneath the salmon in order to hit it.

The Indian, in going from one favorite fishing spot to another on the trail along the river, would hold his spear at the prongs and let the long pole drag along the path behind him.

Old Johnny and his spear pole.

In white man's time the Indian would put sugar on a
roll of salmon eggs and put it out in the sun, claiming the sugar hardened the eggs. The juice in the fresh
eggs would run out when put on a hook, so the Indian
said.

Their baskets, Lillie told me, were made of the roots
of the pine tree, from bears grass, alder roots and the
dark stems of the maidenhair fern. Their patterns de-
picted the phases of nature which especially appealed
to them. She was very adept at the art and her designs
portrayed birds in flight, the markings on their feathers,
animal tracks and lightning. One of her baskets, she
explained to me, bore a pattern of deer droppings.

Gambling played an important role in the life of the
Indian. The Big Straw game and Hand game afforded
much excitement, the dealer waving his arms and sway-
ing and singing to confuse the opponents. I once had
the pleasure of seeing Grant and my husband seated on
the floor of our study, playing the Hand game, with
Lillie, on a chair near by, convulsed with giggling
over their antics.

4   Over Wintu Trails with Laktcharas and Tchitlboole

(Grant and Lillie)

The pleasure of riding and hiking in the mountains and valleys and along the streams of the Trinity, Siskiyou and Shasta region was increased immeasurably when Grant, a native of the area, was able to accompany my husband Pete and me. Familiar spots appeared in an entirely different light when he told us the legends of his forefathers who had lived there, and pointed out the special significance of certain mountain peaks, cliffs and rocks which figured in the stories.

We were shown where the giants lived and the home of the mountain witch who stole children. West of Flume Creek lived a "Supchet," a mean giant. East of Sims at the head of Hazel Creek is a dangerous place, but good spirits live at Mossbrae Falls. Sugarloaf Mountain is a bad place, Grant warned us.

As to the giants, they came out of caves to cast a charm over people. They never had weapons because they were so strong and could kill by crushing their victims. The giants who displeased Olelbes (God) were sent by him to other worlds. The flight of a comet or a falling star was a giant traveling through space.

Grant showed us many locations he called holy places, such as caves, unusual or large rocks, as well as places in rivers or streams where one must be reverential, or where the men would go to pray for strength before a battle or for good luck on a hunt. Such a place was the "bag of bones" on Salt Creek.

One of Grant's favorite anecdotes which he related to

15

others besides us concerned the fate of a white man
from San Francisco who scoffed at the idea of there
being dangerous places in the mountains where one
must be quiet. This man was with a party of others
on a hunting expedition in Shasta County. They had
an Indian by the name of Johnny for a guide.

When they were in the North Salt Creek area Johnny
told them that it was a "bad place" because a half-
coyote, half-wolf spirit lived there and that they must
be quiet. All respected his admonition except the scof-
fer; he was noisy and began to whistle. When the
guide told him it was a "no good place" where they
were about to go the man only laughed and told Johnny
he was too superstitious.

They made camp and then each went his own way to
hunt, agreeing to meet at a certain tree at sundown.
At the end of the day the talkative fellow didn't show
up, Grant told us, so the men went back to look for
him. Finally they found him sitting on a rock and foam-
ing at the mouth! They packed him back to camp and
tried to revive him. Night came on and they made a
fire. The man was breathing but was unconscious.

Johnny, the Indian guide, got some roots -- "charra-
horeed," Grant called it, the leaves of which, he said,
look like carrot tops. The Indian pulverized the roots
and had the fellow inhale the powder, which revived
him.

Grant assured us that on their way home this fellow
was a very quiet person, and a wiser one.

One day in October, 1944, my husband and I took Grant
and Lillie to the former home of Grant's ancestors in
Trinity County. When we reached the site of an old
Wintu dancing lodge in Wintu Gulch below Trinity Center
Grant explained to us how it had formerly looked. Now
all that remained was a slightly raised embankment surrounding a depressed circle in which were now growing
several trees.

We were told that first an earthen ridge six feet high
was made by scooping out the dirt from the center and

piling it around the edge of a fifty-foot circle. Poles
ten feet high were then stuck into the ridge at inter-
vals and then long poles were placed to radiate from
each pole to a higher pole placed in the center. Oak
was used for these posts. The outside of the lodge
was then covered with branches and bark. The entrance was on the south side.

The "dancing feathers" were always kept in the lodge,
he said. During the festivities these feathers, from
hawks, were tied about the ankles and arms of the
dancers for ornament. Dancing was done to the beat
of a stick on wood, a rattle, and to singing and whistling. A fire, when needed, burned near the center of
the lodge as the dancing progressed.

The last "big time" dance there was in 1888 and the
place was abandoned by the Indians in 1890 due to
the influx of whites to their little valley.

As we stood there Grant began to reminisce on those
former happy days when he had attended dances in
1886, '87 and '88. He said that the Indian who had
owned the land at that time was Orlaldolly ("Orlal-
dauli"), which means "tying up." His daughter was
Ida Miller. And an Indian girl named Mary Beech was
always called on to dance first because she was such
a good dancer. Lillie said she went to a dance there
when she was fifteen years old and at that time living
in Chief Alexander's home at Lamoine and at Antler,
and then with her uncle, Jack Hunt. She was an orphan.

We left the site of the lodge and that of a small sweat
house near by, Grant first having expressed his disgust
over the spelling, "Wyntoon," on the sign that had been
placed there, and we drove on to a spot not far from the
bridge over the Trinity River where we picnicked. Rising high above the water on the opposite side we noticed
a peculiar, high cliff with its strata exposed. At once
we saw that Grant was counting the numerous layers or
beds of rock and nodding his head in confirmation of the
number of lines he expected to find there. Then he told
us the following about the place:

The Wintu people call this cliff "Dolomi." Coyote went to the edge of the cliff one early morning and, looking down, saw what he thought was a nice valley, though covered with fog. He did not know that underneath the fog and far below him was a river. He jumped down and was killed on the rocks below! Later, he came back to life and went back to his home, but he did not tell his family what had happened, for he was afraid they would laugh at him.

One of our favorite Coyote stories has for its locale the Stillwater Creek country northeast of Redding and concerns the Buzzard who attempted to build a tower to heaven. While busy at this task, Coyote approached and asked him what he was doing. Hoos, the buzzard, told Sedit, the coyote, that he was building a tower to heaven so folks could see the people up there and get strength from them, and old people could get new life and come back down to earth.

Sedit thought that was a silly thing to do and explained to Hoos that folks had to die lest the earth become overcrowded. With that wise pronouncement he pushed over the tower. Then he saw the buzzard fly away, high up into the sky.

Sedit said, "Wait! Wait! I want to follow you. I'll make myself some wings!"

So he made wings out of sunflower leaves and put them on his arms, Grant said. Then the coyote jumped up and tried to fly, but he could not. He fell back, stunned.

Buzzard came back, saw him and said, "I am going to that mountain east of this place to live. You? I don't know where you will live."

So the mountain, Hoosbooli, is the home of the buzzards, while coyotes live everywhere and have no special home, Grant said. Incidentally, according to Grant, the coyote represents the white man's Lucifer in this story. He said further that the local Indians differ as to the exact location of the buzzard's tower, since there is a somewhat similar formation of boulders

Fallen Stones from the Buzzards Tower

Base of Buzzards Tower

at another spot in the country.

With Grant directing us to the one on Stillwater Creek,
we left the country road and walked a short distance
through a fenced-in field and down to the bank of the
creek. There we saw a huge rock, a smaller one resting on it, and then a line of smaller ones gradating in
size, as they lay on the ground, to a small one at the
end. It did indeed have the appearance of a tower that
had been pushed over. Grant, though knowing of this
location, had never been there before. Seeing it for
the first time, he stood there with his hands on his hips,
looked it over and said, "Yes, looks like human hands
done that." He meant, of course, the buzzard, because of his belief that animals and birds acted like
humans long, long ago.

I once asked my geologist son just what, ages ago,
had caused the interesting arrangement of these boulders. His reply, in geological terms, I have forgotten,
but I remember telling him that I preferred Grant's version.

On another trip we went to the Samwel Cave, in the
Nosoni Creek area in Shasta County, famed for its
story of an Indian girl of long ago who met her death
there by falling far down through an opening in the cave
to the bottom of a lower cavern. A scientific party,
exploring the caves of that area in 1903, made a descent
of the Samwel Cave and discovered the skeleton of the
Indian maiden on the floor of the cavern.*

Grant told us that grizzly bear spirits are supposed to
live in the cave and that it was referred to by the Indians
as "Grizzly Bear Cave." He also mentioned the name
"sar-wol" which means this cave was a holy place
where one could go to get magic strength by bathing in
the pool that was there. It is very probable that the
name "Samwel" (often spelled "Samwell") derived even-
tually from the Wintu "Sar-wol."

_____

*See "The Caves of the Magic Pool," Published Papers and Addresses
of John Campbell Merriam, Carnegie Institution of Washington, D.C.,
1938), III, 1877-1886.

In seeking information about the legend of the Indian
girl I asked Lillie what she knew about it. She said
that all she knew was that three Indian girls went to
an old woman and asked her where they could find a
man. The woman told them to go to this cave to find
a man. Since it was a holy place where men would go
to pray to the Spirits for strength or bravery before a
hunt or a fight, one can see that this would be an apt
place for the maidens to pursue their quest. However,
it resulted in a fatal search for one of them.

Lillie seemed reluctant to say much about it but she
said one of the girls was "the older sister of Abbie
Smith's mother." Abbie Smith was Lillie's aunt with
whom she lived for a time while a young girl, so she
must have often heard the story, but that was all the
information she would give me.

There was still so much to learn from Grant. We should
have had him take us, for example, to the place in the
Sacramento River where lies the white rock that the brave
Indian boys put on top of the giant to hold him down in
the water. We remain ignorant of the location of the
entrance to the underground passage above Sims which
leads up to Mount Shasta and was the home of the giants.
The story of smoking out the giant until the smoke was
seen rising from the mountain prompted us to ask Grant
if his people had ever seen "smoke" coming from Mount
Shasta. He replied that his father had told him that he
had seen "smoke" erupting from the mountain when he
was a very young man living in Trinity. Since Grant
was born in 1873 one could presume that his father was
a young man in the 1850s or perhaps much earlier.

In a meadow near Highway 99 north of Lakehead in
Shasta County Grant showed us a pile of rocks that
his father had told him was the site of a very ancient
earth lodge. Another place we visited -- the location
of an old Indian earth lodge -- is now under the waters
of Lake Shasta, like many of those old homesites.
Grant is gone now, too, and almost all the old Indians
we knew. They who cherished the memories of their
homeland are now fast becoming only memories to us.

Before concluding this already over-extensive intro-
duction to Grant's Wintu legends, I should like to call
attention again to his literary style. The reader will
notice that Grant at times uses modern idioms or the
slang of the white man, expressions which seem in-
congruous, certainly, when related to mythical Indian
personages and happenings. These delightful lin-
guistic anomalies, expressed so unconsciously, make
for us the charm of his stories. No similar amusement
can be derived from the usual Indian myths which have
been collected and published in the interests of ethnology.

A word is necessary in regard to the spelling of the
Indian terms. My husband's mother transcribed many
of Grant's Wintu words in one way, I in another and
Grant produced still a third version. Since none of us
was a linguist trained in the accurate phonetic repre-
sentation of sounds it seemed to me that in this case
it would appear more logical to keep the spelling he
used in his attempt at representing the Wintu sound.
So that is what I have done.

Some students of the language in writing the Wintu
for "God," as an instance, have spelled it "Olelbis."
Grant chose to write it "Olelbes." Another example
is "Torraharsh" for crane, as against "Torihas" and
"Dorehas," the spelling used by other writers of the
Wintu myths.

Grant took such an interest in showing us just how
one's tongue should be placed in order to give the
correct sound to some of his Indian words that it is
unfortunate that his efforts were directed towards such
novices in phonetics as we. It was difficult for us
since so many of the words as he said them came forth
as a sibilance defying transcription. For instance, his
word for lizard, "chi-hwitl," seemed simply a hissing
noise. Whenever I heard him use a word which sounded
hissed, grunted or snorted, I liked to think it was a
holdover from the days long, long ago when, as Grant
firmly believed, "animals talked and acted like human
beings."

Grant's Wintu Legends

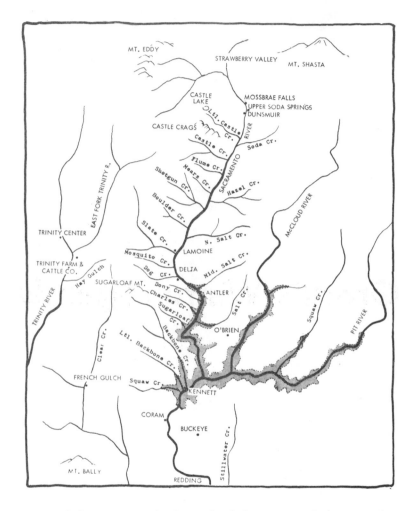

Map of the area in which much of the action of these stories took place. The shaded area is that of the present day Shasta Lake which now covers many of the homesites of those Indians of former days, as does the newly constructed lake in Trinity County, not indicated here.

The Strawberry Valley of old is now the site of the town of Mount Shasta.

5 Grant's Wintu Legends

The Creation of Earth and Its Inhabitants

When Olelbes (One who is up above) created this earth
He put the animals first on the earth and had them act
like people. So these animals lived long time and was
increasing very fast in number, all sizes, big and little.
They were scattered everywhere all over country. These
animals would speak to each other as would a human
being. Sometimes these animals would fight each other
and kill one another. Now Olelbes look down on anil-
mals, saw that they were not getting along good.
Olelbes says to Himself, I will put human being on
earth. So Olelbes put human being on earth, man and
woman. Their color were dark reddish color. Now the
man and woman are having big family.

As the time went by these human being are increasing
very much so some are begin moving out.

It seems that when Olelbes created human being they
were created about the middle of the big land called
Char-le-pom (land of good). When people were increasing in large numbers they were moving towards
south, east and west. Few went north. Those who
went south went clear on to what is now South America
and lived there.

So the reddish or copper-colored race was first created
in North America and South America or Western Hemi-

sphere.

Now Olelbes says to Himself, I am going to make the
animals live more in mountain and hills and human
people more in valley and lowlands near where rivers
and large creeks flow that contains fish so they can
get it and eat it for food.

Now the human people multiplying in great numbers
were fighting among themselves too, like the animals
did before them. But Olelbes look on and didn't bother
them.

It is said that earth was destroyed three different times.
First by fire, next by wind and last by water or flood.
I will write and tell what cause it and by what Being.

First Destroying of Earth by Fire

When Olelbes first put animals and later human beings
on earth it seemed that animals had upper hand yet.
The animals were fighting over things they were getting to eat, especially like fish and dry land game like
deer and others; more so, deer.

Animals built their earth lodges more so on mountains
and hillsides. These animals chose a leader named
Kar'h-kar'h-chee-lah (Adder). He was owner of flint
rock and was furnishing the other animals his flints.

This went on for a long time until one day Adder did
not kill any game. So that night Adder called all the
animals together to talk over for next day's hunt. So
they decided to have game drive from sides of mountain, up through two creeks to a gap.

Adder was the first to start to go up to the gap in the
morning. Adder gave them the poorest kind of flints
he could pick out -- very brittle ones -- taking the
best ones himself.

Next morning they all got up, went down to river, took
bath, came up to their houses, warmed themselves and

ate their meals, then went up to drive the game. They
drove game of all kinds and they killed many deers.
That made the gap run deer-blood down the sides of
the gap. This gap is now called Blood Gap.

This day everybody killed lots of deer but Adder. Now
it made Adder very angry. Adder is thinking now what
to do to get even with them.

Now I know what I will do to get even with them, Adder
says to himself, I will go down south and set a big
forest fire and burn them all up. So that night Adder
sneak off quietly. Being very fast traveler he was gone
far south already. One thing he forgot to take along
was his flints. He left it behind.

Meantime there was band of human people living down
by the river (Sacramento river) on flat on east side of
river. They were called Tu'k.

Next morning the animal inhabitants got up early as
usual but they miss Adder, their leader. Where has
he gone? they says to themselves. And in meantime
somebody spied way to south a thick body of smoke.
Some are now saying it is a forest fire; Adder has gone
south to set fire to forest to burn us up. Some says,
go to his house to see if he took flint rock along. If
he didn't we'll take it and hide it some place where
he will never find it again.

Now they are asking each other who will carry the flint
away and hide it in good place where Adder will never
know. So at last Ground Squirrel says, I will pack it
away to north. All right, they all agreed.

Fox says, I will go up on my mountain, look south and
tell you how close the forest fire is coming up. But
Fox mountain, being very low mountain, Fox could not
see very far south. So Sandhill Crane says, I will go
up on my mountain, which is higher than your mountain,
and from there on top I will look south and tell our
friend, Ground Squirrel, how close the forest fire is
coming up.

So now the ground squirrel packs the flint on his back, goes north with it.

Ground Squirrel travel, travel for long time. Every once in a while he would holler and Sandhill Crane would say, go on little farther north.

Ground Squirrel travel and travel and finally he came to a point just little east of Bohem Puyuik (Mt. Shasta). There he stopped and hollered but he heard no answer. So he says to himself, this must be the place. I'll leave this flint here and call this Flint mountain. And also I will leave a guardian just little to southwest near foot of Bohem Puyuik, a woman called Tho-uk (worm).

All that was left behind all burn up, including human people.

Right at present time there is form resembling like human laying all toward up hill. And the ground squirrel -- he has a black mark on his back to this day where flint dirt had rubbed on him.

This finish story so I quit.

The woman guardian that Ground Squirrel placed on the eastern slope of Mount Shasta.

Second Destroying of Earth

Long, long ago there lived lots of Indians on McCloud River, place called Wy-el-num-mel-taus. Among those Indians there was one big chief, very rich man, who had two sons and one very beautiful looking daughter. One of the sons -- older one -- was a great gambler, and the younger son, a great hunter of game.

This older son went down south country to gamble with people there. He took along with him some fine beads to bet with. This being about spring of year. He travel and travel, winning lots of bets. So he began to turn homeward. On way home he lost what he had won and now began to lose his own beads. He now stays in one place and bets all his bets from long distance saying, I'll so and so, and if I lose you go to my father and collect from him what I have lost; he will let you have it.

Finally, chief's older son gambled away all he had and started home. When the gambler came home his father, the chief, told his son, saying, why don't you go to a holy spring and pray for good luck? But his son did not pay any attention to him but went on gambling with what his mother had given him to gamble with. He lost all that and come home once more.

This time the old chief, his father, was very angry. He told again to his gambling son, why don't you do something for yourself if you are to continue to gamble? I say, you go to some holy spring or some place and pray for your luck.

Day was getting toward afternoon and so when supper time came the young man's mother told her son to eat, but he said he didn't want to eat.

When evening time came the gambling son picked up piece of burning wood for torch, walks out of earth lodge and leaves, going toward west. Pretty soon his younger brother caught up with him and he said, I am going with you, brother.

No, said the older brother, you had better not. I am
going long ways.

But the younger brother said, never mind; let me go
with you so we can look after each other.

So they went west up Herz creek, over Lac-chim-soo-
ba-we-les divide, west, crossed Salt Creek, west to
little valley called Charrowkota, west over Tobaskalai,
down toward Sacramento river, cross the river at place
now called Antler and went up the river little way and
came to bend just east of Smithson Flat. It was getting
along night now; was dark. Older brother says, let's
build fire first and I can go in swim in water pretty soon.
So they build fire and older brother says, I am going to
swim now; you stay here at fire.

No, I will follow you, said the younger brother. So
they went in the river and swam out on rock. Older
brother told younger one, you stay on this rock while
I dive down in this deep water-hole. So younger brother
sat on rock waiting for him long time. Finally older
brother come up toward surface. It was getting toward
morning. Just then the morning star rise up over east
mountains. They went out on shore, build some fire,
warm themselves and lay down. Both went to sleep
right away. Soon they both woke up. It was getting
almost daybreak and light now. Older brother said,
did you dream anything? Younger brother said, yes, I
dreamed that wind was blowing so hard on one of the
pine trees that it snapped off and fell near me. And
younger brother said to his older brother, did you dream
anything?

Yes, said older brother, I dreamed that there was a cold
north wind blowing so hard that it uproot the trees and
was blowing them away.

So now it is day. They go back to their father and
mother and sister on McCloud river. Got there little
after sunrise. Mother tells them to eat their breakfast. Younger brother ate but older brother, the gambler, did not eat; just went and lay down in bed in their
earth lodge.

Now it is commence to blow cold north wind. What
was nice warm summer now is turning cold weather.
All at once people are wondering what has gone wrong.
All people had better gather in earth lodges, stay in,
have Indian doctor find out what was wrong with weather.
They ask the two brothers if they know anything, but
they held back awhile. Finally, when the wind was
blowing harder, younger brother said, me and my older
brother went and swimmed in holy water last night and
dreamed that there was strong north wind blowing.
Blowed everything away.

When the people heard this they said to themselves,
world is coming to an end. They went in their earth
lodges. Few went to mountain caves to save themselves, but ones that went in earth lodges were all
destroyed. Last earth lodge held out was the big earth
lodge big chief lived in. It blowed away last.

So this end this story. I finish.

Story of Harkummintakona, the Long Tail Man

Third and Last Destroy of Earth

The long tail people came into being at place called
Charrownoral on Trinity river on west bank of river
just west of present day Trinity Farm and Cattle Company's place near Trinity Center. They were all young
people, big and tall with long tail. No one know how
and where they came from; they talk and act much different than other people. Although they hunted wild game
as other people did they did not associate with them.
They build themselves a big earth lodge to live in.
They lived for long time and was increasing very fast
with their families.

Now there was one person with these long tail people
acted much more odd than the others; he was living in
his earth lodge by himself. This one would lay down
most all day; only time he get up was when mealtime
came around.

The other people never visit these long tail people;
they kept themselves away from them, all together.
They did not like them at all.

Now, one that was doing something strange, he is now
pounding dirt with his elbow, using one hand to throwing dirt in his mouth. Now the other people with long
tail heard what he was doing; they were all afraid, saying, he is pounding dirt with his elbow; we will call
him Harkummintakona (pounding with elbow). Meanwhile Olelbes was looking down, saw Harkummintakona
what he was doing. So Olelbes decided to punish these
people for doing no good. So Olelbes says to Himself
I will make flood come and drown all these people down
there.

Now Olelbes made wind blow and bring clouds and rain
and floods. Meantime other people with no tail were
preparing to get away from the floods. Some were making rafts and canoe boats and some big baskets. Even
the animals were working too, such as beavers and
otters and even such small animals as gophers and
moles. Beaver and otter were building the dam, and
also the little mole was helping them, too. Beaver
and otter had mole to hold the support from lower side;
that's what made the mole's hands bend back wide open
to this day. The gopher was told to make many holes
so that water would drain.

Now the rain was coming down so much that the water
sprouted out of the ground everywhere all around the
lowland filling up creeks and rivers very fast. The
people that knew where there was a cave way up on
some high mountains, those went there and were save
from drowning, but those that stayed back and tried to
save themselves on rafts and canoes were all drowned.
Some animals saved themselves by going up on high
mountains too.

Now Harkummintakona was laying in his earth lodge
asleep when water began coming in on him. He tried
to get up but he could not move. His arm that was
used for pounding dirt was sunk down deep into ground
and his body tied down to ground. During his sleep
some of his people had tied him down during the night

just before the flood appeared.

Now Harkummintakona struggled hard and got himself free and stood up, found himself standing in water to his knees. Inside his earth lodge he said to himself that water out there is not going to drown me; I will get out of here and get away safe. So Harkummintakona walk to the earth lodge door, open it and walk out and saw that the flood was coming everywhere deep, but to him it only came up to his knees.

Now Harkummintakona pick up little black bird and start walking out. Now Olelbes saw what Harkummintakona was doing against his ruling of the people on earth. So Olelbes took out his slingshot and began to throw rocks with his slingshot with his left arm. So now Olelbes was called Numthalestawa (throwing with left hand). He would throw at Harkummintakona. It would strike him on his shoulders or back, would just glance off, making like a ringing noise. When he was hit he would say "chokee, chokee, chokee, chokee."

Now Olelbes was throwing at every human in sight. Now Harkummintakona was wading up toward northeast, water only up to his knees all the time. Now Harkummintakona was left all by himself and the little black bird he saved; was carrying it under his armpit. Harkummintakona was taking the little black bird name Cha-cha-cha-ot for company. Now Harkummintakona and the little black bird are wading toward northeast very fast. It seems that no matter how hard or how often he was hit with rocks by slingshot it did not hurt him. By moving fast in wading through water Harkummintakona is nearly out of sight, going pretty well toward east now, still saying "chokee, chokee, chokee, chokee."

Now Harkummintakona and his little black bird called Cha-cha-cha-ot which he took along with him for company are gone out of sight.

Now Harkummintakona and the little black bird are supposed to go to place called Po-kus-poi-hor-e-pom (country of dry land) and there end his life on this earth.

This is all. I finish.

Story of Norwanchakas and Keriha

Norwanchakas and Keriha came to being near the foot
of southeast of Num-mel-be-le-sas-pom (west uphill
burning place), now called Mt. Eddy. Their parents
were of common being. When Norwanchakas and Keriha
were little boys they went out and played by themselves;
they would not play with other children. Norwanchakas'
and Keriha's father soon taught them how to use bow and
arrow.

Norwanchakas and Keriha began to grow fast and were
now grown into young manhood; so their father made
them stout bow and nice strong arrows with best of
flint, and some red flint to shoot bears with, especially the grizzly bears.

Now the people around them are taking notice of these
two young brothers. Norwanchakas was older and Keriha
younger. They were very handsome young fellows, very
large and powerful men, Norwanchakas being taller.
Although their parents were common being, the two
young men, Norwanchakas and Keriha, told their father
they had better build them a new big earth lodge so they
can live in nice warm house in winter. All right, go
ahead, said their father. So Norwanchakas and Keriha
went to work to build a big, nice earth lodge.

Now Norwanchakas and Keriha and their parents are
being known far and wide by other peoples because
these two young men could do what others could not
do, such as go out and hunt and kill lots of game, say,
one or two big fat bucks, one big bear, one big elk,
one or five antelope, and smaller game, and pack them
all on their backs and bring them all to the earth lodge
for their father and mother to eat. When outside tribes
made war on their people, Norwanchakas and Keriha
was always called on to help them to fight and they
always came out victor. So these people lived that
way for long time until everybody became peaceable.

Now Norwanchakas and his brother Keriha was hunting
far down south on Num-tee-pom-all-way-nem (west
place up stream: Sacramento river). They met a man
one day. The man told them that he had been down south
on this same river, way down place called Bar-ras.
Being now summertime the fish in river down there were
running, lots of them, the man told Norwanchakas and
Keriha. Yes, said Norwanchakas and Keriha to the man;
and the man goes on his way home, leaving them where
he met them.

Now when Keriha, the younger brother, heard all this
going on down south at Bar-ras he wanted to go down
there right away. He say to his older brother, let's
go down there now from here. Let's not go home first.
No, said Norwanchakas, the older brother, we must
first tell our father and mother where we are going.
So they returned home that afternoon and told their
father and mother what they heard that day from man
who had been down south catching fish with other people
down there.

Keriha, the younger brother, was so anxious to go down
south he did not sleep that night; but Norwanchakas
slept good all night and got up early next morning,
went to the river, which was west fork of Sacramento
river, and took his morning bath. Little later Keriha,
younger brother, comes down to the river, takes his
morning bath, too. They go back to the earth lodge,
eat their breakfast.

Now Norwanchakas and Keriha got ready to go down
south. They made them each nice spear poles. Keriha
is restless, wants to go in hurry, but Norwanchakas,
the older brother, takes his time; tells his younger
brother don't be in hurry, we'll be down there among
those people very soon enough; you will find lots to
do, maybe.

It was still early yet in the morning so the two brothers,
Norwanchakas and Keriha, bid their father and mother
goodby, this being the first time the two brothers are
going away so far from their people.

They traveled all day until sundown. They came to place

called Hee-in-pom (now called Lamoine). There they
found lots of people, the place being a large ranchería.
There was a large earth lodge where the chief lived.
They came and met the two brothers, Norwanchakas
and Keriha. The two brothers told the people their
names and who they were. All the people were glad
to meet them. They all said we have heard of you two
brothers already; you are two wonderful men; you two
will be treated as our family. We have heard down
south at place called Bar-ras people there are catching
lots of fish and we are going down there tomorrow.
Won't you young fellows go down with us tomorrow?

Sure, we will go with you. We have never been down
there. We are strangers. We will be very glad to go
south with you.

So next morning very early the chief gets up and tells
his people to get up, be ready to travel down south
to big gathering. So they all got up early, took their
morning bath, came back to the house, ate their
breakfast and was ready to travel. He tells some of
his men to stay home. And now chief says ready,
people, let's go.

So they travel all day. They cross the Sacramento
river at Mo-nok-chee-row, once called Kennett, followed down the river about five miles on east side of
river, came to the big gathering place where they
were catching fish of all sizes from riffle pike up to
big sturgeon.

Now the head chief at the gathering place got up and
began making a speech, which is custom for chief
to do when other chief and his people come to his
place. Now the chief at the gathering place stops
talking. The chief from north now makes his speech,
telling them he had along with him two brothers, their
names are Norwanchakas and Keriha.

When the chief and his people at the gathering place
heard Norwanchakas' and Keriha's names they was
very glad that they had come. They said, we have
heard of these two brothers already. We was told
how great they are.

Now night coming on, they all go to bed for night.
Next morning early the chief at the gathering place
got up first and made his morning speech and soon
stopped. And now the chief from north began make
his big talk and soon stops. By now everybody is
getting up for the day. Norwanchakas and Keriha
get up and go down to the river, take their morning
bath, come back to the gathering place. Now it is
breakfast time. They all eat their breakfast. Norwanchakas and Keriha looked around and it seemed
to them everywhere they looked they could see lots
of dried fish strung up on poles.

Now, says Keriha to his brother Norwanchakas in
whisper, we will have lots of fun catching fish with
those people; we'll fish for them and load them down
all we can; we'll show them we can catch more fish
than they can all together.

No, don't be foolish, said Norwanchakas, they may
be better fishermen than we are. So now they all go
down to the fishing ground, some to fishing house
and some to boil fishing. Norwanchakas and Keriha
follows the crowd and looks on from the shore; sees
the people from gathering place fish first. Keriha
can hardly keep himself still. Every now and then
he whispers to his brother Norwanchakas, I want to
fish. But Norwanchakas says to him wait awhile,
you will have a chance pretty soon.

By now it is getting along middle of forenoon and
people from gathering place are catching lots of fish
of all sizes from little salmon to great big sturgeons.
Now the chief from gathering place tells his men to
stop fishing and gather up all the fish, take it to the
gathering place to have it cooked for lunch. Let's
treat our visitors to some fish to eat.

Keriha says to his brother Norwanchakas, let's pack
some fish for them. But his brother Norwanchakas
says no, not now. Wait 'til this afternoon. So the
people from the gathering place carry all the fish.

Now the cooks, who are mostly women, are busy
cooking all around the gathering place. Then they

bring all they cooked and place it on ground under large shade tree; there was plenty of acorn soup, too.

The chief from gathering place gets up and tells the chief from north, come and have something to eat and this afternoon my men will fish some more for you to take home tomorrow. So the chief from north tells his host, come, let's eat.

After they had their dinner the chief from north make his speech and ends his talk by telling the chief at gathering place, my men will fish for you people this afternoon. So they all go down to the river to the fishing ground. Keriha is getting very anxious to fish but his brother Norwanchakas tells him to take his time. So now they begin to fish. Some go to fish house, some to boils. Norwanchakas and Keriha pick out one boil and commence to fish. The people from gathering place are looking on. The people from north who were at station down stream from Norwanchakas and Keriha were catching fish already so they hollered to the brothers they had missed some and to watch out for them to come by up there.

Pretty soon Norwanchakas got one and also brother Keriha got one; and from then on they caught many fish. Soon they had the shore near them piled up so deep with fish they had to quit. The two brothers, Norwanchakas and Keriha, catch most of the fish, never losing one, while other men from north lost many big fish, mostly sturgeons. Norwanchakas and Keriha pull out many big sturgeon.

Now the two brothers tell the people from gathering place who were looking on, tells them, pack all you can and we'll pack the rest. All goes back to gathering place. One of them who was first to get to gathering place tells to the two chiefs, one from gathering place and one from north, we have never seen like way those two brothers, Norwanchakas and Keriha, can fish. Why, they have already caught fish enough for us all next winter.

They all put down their loads of fish. The chiefs notice that there was no sturgeon; they were all sal-

mons! Where are the two brothers, Norwanchakas
and Keriha, said the two chiefs. They are back down
there coming with their load, the people said.

Pretty soon the two brothers, Norwanchakas and Keriha, comes with their load, puts it down on ground.
Everybody, all 'round, looked at the two brothers,
Norwanchakas and Keriha, how powerful they were,
for they had packed all the many sturgeons and the
many large salmons they had caught which the other
fellows had left for them to pack.

The day being in afternoon the chief from the gathering place gets up, makes his talk and ends in telling the chief from north that his men had caught e-
nough fish for just now and you are going back tomorrow so we will keep the fresh fish and we will
give you dried ones we already got, which is easy
to carry.

All that afternoon and way into night the people at
the gathering place is talking about those two brothers, Norwanchakas and Keriha, how they could
catch so many fish in one short afternoon. Some
says, yes, it would take us all here at gathering
place all this summer and clear into fall to catch as
many as they did this afternoon; those two brothers
are sure great young men! Just think, every time
they spear at one they sure gets them; they never
miss or lose one.

Next morning, bright and early, the two brothers,
Norwanchakas and Keriha, get up and go down to
river, take their morning bath, come back to the gathering place. The chief from the gathering place gets
up now and makes his morning speech and tells the
chief from the north to come bring your people and
eat breakfast, you are going travel on your way home
north today. So people eats their breakfast, finish,
and now the chief from north makes his farewell
speech to chief at gathering place and says we will
leave you people, hoping you will all be well when
we come down again.

Do come down again. Bring those two young men,
Norwanchakas and Keriha; they are our friends. They
are welcome to be with us down here anytime they
come here.

So now the people from north start home northward.
They come up same trail they had travel down, cross
the Sacramento river at Mo-nok-chee-row (Kennett).
They are traveling same speed as when they were
traveling south, without load. Now they come to
Hee-in-pom (Lamoine) about sundown. Everybody
who was left behind at home were very glad to see
them back. And now the chief is making his speech
to his people who were left at home, telling them how
good they were treated by the chief and his people
down south at the gathering place, telling them we
must go down there again soon; they are good people
down there.

Now the people who were left at home by the chief
had supper ready when they came home and all ate
supper. Little while after supper the chief gets up,
makes his speech for night, and tells ones who were
down south at the gathering place to lay down and
rest up for the night, especially the two brothers
Norwanchakas and Keriha, who were still to travel
home northward next morning.

Early next morning Norwanchakas and Keriha got up
and went down east to the river, took their morning
bath, came back to the rancheria. The chief was in
his earth lodge. By now everybody is getting up.
The chief now gets up, comes outside of his earth
lodge, makes his early morning speech, and now tells
his people to give his two young friends, Norwanchakas and Keriha, their breakfast, for they are going to
travel long ways today. Norwanchakas and his brother Keriha ate their breakfast, got through and was now
ready to start. Norwanchakas made farewell speech
to the chief and his people, thanking them for taking
them along down south to gathering place.

Now Norwanchakas and Keriha leave for home, to
their father and mother's home to north at foot of
southeast of Num-mel-be-le-sas-pom (Mt. Eddy).

They travel all day although they both had big load of dried salmon. They traveled same speed as they did going south with no load.

Now Norwanchakas and Keriha is home. Their father and mother are very glad to see them home because they were very worried; their sons had made first trip into strange country and they thought they may have some trouble traveling around the country.

Now the father of Norwanchakas and Keriha is calling his people to come to his earth lodge, get some dried salmon that his sons had bring home from down south on their trip down there. Everybody is very glad to see those two brothers, Norwanchakas and Keriha. So now everybody had all the dried salmon they want to eat because they had no chance to get big fish like salmon; only little brook trout they could catch in brooks of mountains.

So now, year after year, the people of Norwanchakas and Keriha go down south to the big gathering place at Bar-ras to fish. Going down, they always stop at Hee-in-pom (Lamoine) where their former friend, the chief, lives. And the chief and his people always go down south with them and always travel in peace long as the chief was with them.

One day on one of these trips at the gathering place Norwanchakas and Keriha was told that there was a young man who lives down south up flat called East Gap. They say he is very short man but has wonderful strength for his size. His name is Nordalmunoko. When Norwanchakas and Keriha heard that name they said he is our cousin; we would like to see him very much. So the chief at the gathering place send one man to tell Nordalmunoko to come to fishing gathering place. Pretty soon the man comes back, tells them that Nordalmunoko will come tomorrow, be here at forenoon.

When Norwanchakas and Keriha heard the news they were very glad; they were very anxious to see their cousin. Now Keriha says to his brother Norwanchakas we'll show Nordalmunoko how to fish when he comes.

Don't fool yourself; he may show us how to fish, himself, said his brother, Norwanchakas.

So next day most of fishermen went down to river to
fish. Only the chiefs and the womenfolks who was
the main cooks and some menfolks who gathered wood
for fire and Keriha stayed at the gathering place in
their camping house.

Before Nordalmunoko leave his place his grandmother
filled in his net bag all the potatoes she could fill,
but it only showed to fill just one corner of the net
bag. So now Nordalmunoko starts on his way to gathering place. It didn't take him long to get there.
When Nordalmunoko was nearing the gathering place
he looked straight ahead. He sees a nice looking
camp house. Now he stopped and looked some more.
He thought to himself that must be a chief's camp
house. So he left his net bag of potatoes and went
to the camp house, knocks on the door, went in. He
saw a mighty handsome and powerful looking young
man before him. It was Keriha who he saw now for
the first time. So Keriha looks at the little man, Nordalmunoko, and asks him where he came from and how
far he traveled that day.

Nordalmunoko said I came only short distance. I
came to see my two cousins, Norwanchakas and Keriha. I was told they had come down from north to fish.

Yes, says Keriha, you stay here and wait. I will go
down to river where the people are fishing. And he
walks out of camp house, never telling Nordalmunoko
who he was. So when Keriha got down to the river
where Norwanchakas was fishing he told them that
their cousin, Nordalmunoko, had come; says he is
a little fellow. I am going to have a lot of fun with
him.

You had better not fool with him, says his brother,
Norwanchakas. I understand he is very powerful man.

So Keriha goes back up to the camp house and finds

Nordalmunoko waiting for him. The day was still early in forenoon. So little while after Keriha came back from the river Nordalmunoko tells Keriha he had put down on ground a little net bag of potatoes; would Keriha go and get it? Soon Keriha comes back without potatoes. Tells Nordalmunoko he could not lift it.

Why, what's the matter? said Nordalmunoko to Keriha, I carried it from my home here. It is not heavy. Come, see me carry it for you. So they went out together. Nordalmunoko picked it up with one hand, took it into the camp house.

Now Keriha was so surprised he did not know what to say. Keriha looked and looked at Nordalmunoko for a while, wondering how he could be so strong for a little man.

The day is still forenoon yet, but the fishermen are coming in with their fish and last one comes in is Norwanchakas with his big load of fish.

Hello, says Norwanchakas to Nordalmunoko. Our cousin, I am glad to see you. We will catch some fish for you to take home this afternoon. All right, said his cousin, I would like to get some fish to take home.

So now noontime comes and everyone is eating their dinner. They finish their dinner and are resting awhile before they go to fishing. After awhile, before they go to fishing, the chief at the gathering place gets up, makes his daily speech, tell all the people that Nordalmunoko has come to see us all, now we must treat him good because he is cousin to our friends, Norwanchakas and Keriha. You fishermen catch some fish for him to take home.

So now all the fishermen goes down to the river. Nordalmunoko is traveling down to the river with his two cousins, Norwanchakas and Keriha, who are the last ones to get down to the fishing place. Now every fisherman is ready to fish, but little Nordalmunoko is just looking on. Pretty soon Keriha ask Nordalmunoko if he would like to fish. He thinks it would be lot of

fun to see Nordalmunoko fish because he is so little.
If he catches any of the big sturgeon he will be pulled
in the river sure. He never thinks what he saw him do
about that net bag of potatoes.

After Keriha asked Nordalmunoko, his cousin, about
three times and handed him his spear pole, Nordalmunoko said, I got spear pole of my own; I will use it.
So he pulls out a nice spear pole and about twenty
pairs of toggles and told Norwanchakas and Keriha,
his cousins, to take off the toggles soon as he catches
a fish.

All right, go ahead and fish, says Keriha. He was
now very glad to see Nordalmunoko fish.

Now, all this time Norwanchakas, the older brother,
who was taller of the two brothers, never ask his
cousin Nordalmunoko to fish or do other things. He
knew already that Nordalmunoko could do 'most anything over anybody when anything was going on. But
Keriha always like to have fun with everybody, not
meaning harm but just fun.

So now Nordalmunoko began to fish. First one he
caught was very big salmon; then comes very large
sturgeon. He pulled it out like it was a little fish.

Now Nordalmunoko is catching fish of all kinds, just
right and left, keeping Norwanchakas and Keriha, his
cousins, very busy. Although the sun is high in afternoon Keriha says to his brother, Norwanchakas, let's
tell Nordalmunoko to stop fishing for he has caught
enough fish for this season already. He is keeping
us busy taking his toggles off the fish; we cannot
keep up with him. So Norwanchakas tells his cousin,
Nordalmunoko, to stop fishing. All right, says Nordalmunoko, I was just beginning to fish good, but if
you say so, I will quit.

Now they are loading themselves with the fish that
Nordalmunoko caught. They made three trips to the
gathering place but only took away about one fourth
fish that was piled up on the river bank. Nordalmunko
told them to take all they can. So they made three

more trips and they said, it is enough; we got all we
can take care of for this season, and they left him
half the pile of fish.

So now Nordalmunoko loads himself up. He takes
his net bag, puts all fish in net bag, throws it over
his shoulder, walks up toward the gathering place.
He stops for few minutes and tells the chief at gathering place and the chief from the north goodby, will
see you again soon, and moves on toward his home
to East Gap on south up flat.

Now all the people are wondering how that little man,
Nordalmunoko, could pack such a big load, make it
look so little he could pick it up easy when others
could not do it. So that evening the chief at the gathering place made his evening speech telling them now
you have all seen greatest fisherman in this country,
our friend Nordalmunoko. He is wonderful man; he
can do 'most anything, I believe.

So next morning the chief from north gets up early and
tells his people to get up. So they all got up. Norwanchakas and Keriha get up, go down to river to take
their morning bath and come back up to the gathering
place. All eat their breakfast and now are ready to
start for home to north. The chief from north now gets
up and makes his farewell speech to the chief at the
gathering place; and now they leave the gathering
place, always traveling same trail up the Num-tee-
pom-all-way-nem (west place up stream: Sacramento
river). They all got home up north safe at Hee-in-
pom. Soon as they got home they were told right
away that there was a Supchet (giant) staying at place
called Ho-yo-kee-pom (whistling place) and he is
killing anybody he sees going up or down the river.
Have you seen him?

No, said the chief, we never saw him on our way
down or back up.

The people who were down at Ho-yo-kee-pom being
few in company were caught by this Supchet and killed, so we are told. Since you all went down to the
big gathering place he has killed many as ten people

already. When he kills his victim he takes its heart
out and carries the body, taking it to west.

So all that night everybody kept awake. Next morn-
the two brothers, Norwanchakas and Keriha, went to
river to take their morning bath. Keriha said to his
brother Norwanchakas, let's go back down and see
this Supchet.

No, said Norwanchakas. My brother, let's go on up
home to our father and mother; tell them and other
people what we heard about that Supchet, what he is
doing to the people down there. Then we can come
back down here and take along few of these men here
with us so they can witness whatever takes place.

So the two brothers, Norwanchakas and Keriha, gets
ready to start for their home north, bid farewell to the
chief and start on their way home. They didn't see
anybody on the way because lots of people heard that
this Supchet was traveling up and down but lately
stayed at place called Ho-yo-kee-pom and had killed
many people.

The two brothers got home safe and their father and
mother were very glad to see them home all right.
First thing the father and mother ask them was if they
had seen that Supchet who was killing lots of people,
who is staying on the trail, place called Ho-yo-kee-
pom.

No, we haven't seen him yet, but when we got back
to Hee-in-pom with the chief and his people, back
from the gathering place, we were told that the Supchet was waylaying lots of people. When he kills
one he takes out its heart and carries the body and
takes it towards west.

Next morning the two brothers, Norwanchakas and
Keriha, went down the river which is west fork of
Sacramento river, took their early morning bath, came
to earth lodge, ate their breakfast in a hurry, finish,
and now tell their father and mother they are going
down to Hee-in-pom and have a talk with the chief
down there what to do with that Supchet who is at

Ho-yo-kee-pom. Now we are going down this morning. If we are killed by that Supchet we won't be the
only ones; we will have somebody to go along with
us; we have good friend, the chief at Hee-in-pom.
He will let us take some of his men, I am sure.

So that morning the two brothers, Norwanchakas and
Keriha, bid their father and mother and all the people
goodby and left them behind, telling them not to worry. The two brothers were very anxious to see that
Supchet. It took them only half a day to get down to
Hee-in-pom this time. When the two brothers got
there they found all the people were very excited and
all were talking about that Supchet because he had
killed some of their people. They were planning how
to meet the Supchet.

Pretty soon the two brothers, Norwanchakas and Keriha, got a chance to talk to the chief. They told the
chief they had better go down and meet him tomorrow.
We would like to have some of your picked men go
with us, they said. All right, said the chief. So
that night they held a war council against the Supchet.

Next morning as usual Norwanchakas and Keriha got
up early, went down to the river, took their morning
baths. After getting out on shore Norwanchakas held
up his hands and prayed to Olelbes to help him to
punish this giant who is killing lots of people at Ho-
yo-kee-pom. After finish praying they come back to
the earth lodge where the chief was staying. They
all ate their breakfast, finish, and now was ready
to start. The chief picked out twenty of the best
fighters he had and the chief says to his men, you
must follow these two brothers, Norwanchakas and
Keriha; do what they tell you to do. You must take
their orders.

The day is still early. It is not yet sunrise. They
start on their way to Ho-yo-kee-pom. They all are
traveling very fast. They come to place called Cho-
pus (wading place). There they ford the Sacramento
river (near present Southern Pacific railroad tunnel
number five) and went on down to gap called "whistling gap," (just west of Southern Pacific railroad

tunnel number four), then little to northwest of Ho-
yo-kee-pom. Here Norwanchakas and Keriha tells
the chief's men to stay back while the two brothers
go on down, telling them to be in their sight all the
time.

So now the two brothers, Norwanchakas and Keriha,
go on ahead. They didn't go very far when they saw
the giant coming up toward them. The two brothers
walk on. Pretty soon the Supchet saw the two brothers, Norwanchakas and Keriha. He stopped and waited for them. The two brothers hurry on and soon they
are beside the Supchet. The Supchet looks at the two
brothers, sizes them up and says to them, where are
you two going?

Norwanchakas answers the Supchet (Norwanchakas is
doing all the talking and Keriha keeping still). We
are going south to big gathering place long way down
south.

You are not, said the giant. This is far south you
will go. In saying so, the Supchet grabs Norwanchakas and tries to strangle Norwanchakas. But Norwanchakas was too quick for the Supchet. Norwanchakas
trip and swung the Supchet so swift he fell face down
so hard he struck his head on rock; he busted his head
and was killed by Norwanchakas singlehanded. (There
used to be a large footprint and large man's chest print
on flat rock, but when the railroad was built up the
Sacramento river canyon the foot and chest prints were
covered with rock, gravel and dirt so that it cannot be
seen now). The head ornament that the giant wore
fell off his head and left a monument which you can
see to this day.*

Now Norwanchakas and Keriha drags the dead giant
to a deep hole in the Sacramento river. Norwanchakas tells his brother Keriha to go and tell the chief's

*This rock, however, which Grant had pointed out to us, was knocked
over when a change on State highway 99 was made several years ago.

men to come and help sink the dead giant in deep hole. So now all go and gather large rocks but they could not sink the dead giant; it always comes to top. Finally Norwanchakas tells his brother Keriha and all the chief's men who are with them to go west to Wy-kee-dee-pom (leaning north place), there get one large boulder rock, bring it here. So they went to Wy-kee-dee-pom. There they got one white boulder and put it on the dead Supchet's body and sunk it down. It did not come up any more, this time. The white rock can be seen in the Sacramento river to this day. Only white rock around there. So now Norwan-chakas had killed the Supchet singlehanded. Everybody was now safe, so they all went home north, safe and sound.

The two brothers, Norwanchakas and Keriha, on their way home, stops and tells the chief at Hee-in-pom what they had done to the Supchet. And the chief was very glad to hear the news.

Now Norwanchakas and Keriha make their farewell speech to the chief and go on to their home up foot of southeast of Num-mel-be-le-sas-pom. There they lived long time and end their days on this earth.

This ends this story. I finish.

Story of Nordalmunoko

Long, long ago lots of Indian people lived at place called Mohmas just north of present town of Redding. There was one family there who had big earth lodge and all around this big earth lodge lots of Indians lived. In this big earth lodge there was a child born, little baby boy. (He was born on what became known in the white man's time as the Diestelhorst ranch, north Redding, near the Sacramento river bridge.).

When the child cried his cry sounded like little cub bear crying, so his father named him Nordalmunoko.

The little baby Nordalmunoko cried so much people

were getting afraid of him, even his own father and
mother. So one day, being at springtime of year,
all people decided to go east toward what is now Cow
creek country to dig potatoes and get clover and
greens, leaving baby Nordalmunoko behind them, all
by himself, crying all the time. So, soon after all
were out of his sight, little baby Nordalmunoko gets
up on his feet, walks toward north, his baby basket
tied on his back. He goes over hill, north, cross
Sulphur creek, goes northeast, comes to Boulder
creek. Here he stops, takes off his baby basket,
puts it away under brush. The baby Nordalmunoko
is growing very fast now. He looks all over country. Looks once more toward east; looks toward Cow
creek and says to himself, I am going wish for big
rain-shower. So the big rain-shower came. He hid
himself in brush where he had left his baby basket.
Sat there all day.

He wish this rain because his father and mother and
sister and all the people had deserted him. He wanted
them to get soaking wet. So that evening everybody
came home soaking wet, including baby Nordalmunoko's father, mother and sister. They did not find the
baby they had left behind. It now getting toward
night, everybody was out looking for the baby. They
could only find some sign of tracks once in a while.
They hunted for him all night.

So meantime Nordalmunoko is growing quite big boy;
is making himself at home feeding on clover and
greens. He moves farther northeast and comes to a
a nice flat just east of little creek; there he stop and
sits down. While sitting there, all at once a white
ball rolled to his side. He picked it up and put it to
his mouth. It tasted good to him. He ate it all up.

Next day his sister, who had been looking for him
all this time, found him. She had basket of potatoes
to feed her young brother. She told him to go back
home with her, but he refused, so she went home a-
lone, crying.

That evening, when his sister left him, a red-looking
ball rolled to his side. He looked at it a while, pick-

ed it up and put it to his mouth. It tasted good to
him so he ate it all up. Now, these two red and white
balls were one of salt and one of full ripe cherry.

Then, that same evening he saw an old woman coming
toward him. The boy, Nordalmunoko, watch. Soon
old woman comes up to him, says hello, Grandson.
I been told you were lost; now I find you, my grandson. I already send you nice ball of salt and nice,
full ripe cherry. This place where I find you will be
called East Salt Flat, and your nickname will be Nor-
dalwelimuk, meaning south salt flat man.

So his grandmother told him to go with her now that
he was all alone, but Nordalmunoko said no, not now.
My sister is coming to see me tomorrow; I want to
see her once more. So old grandmother went home
alone that evening.

Next day Nordalmunoko's sister came with food for
her brother and told him once more to go home with
her but her brother said no, I am going home with my
grandmother who came to see me yesterday. Tell my
father and mother I am not coming home. I am not
coming to them. So his sister left him, going back
home alone, crying. Next day his grandmother comes
and takes him home with her, place call Puyalkalai
(east gap) west of Buckeye creek. There they lived.
Young Nordalmunoko is growing fast to boyhood. His
grandmother makes him a bow and arrows to shoot
birds with. Every day he goes out and hunts and kills
lots of birds.

Then Nordalmunoko grows to young manhood and his
grandmother makes another bow and some arrows,
bigger and stouter, nice looking bow and arrows. Now
he hunts for big game like deer, bear and antelope.

One day his grandmother tells him that there is something stealing the acorns she has left in creek to soak;
says it takes even the basket. So Nordalmunoko takes
his bow and arrows, goes down to deep water in
creek, waits for the thing that was stealing his grandmother's soaked corn. Pretty soon he saw something
move toward the basket of acorns. He looked at it

good, first, then took aim and shot. It went down
in water. Pretty soon it came up on top of water,
dead, near where he stood. He saw it was fine big
otter. Nordalmunoko took it out of water, skinned
it and took it home to his grandmother.

So they live this way for long time; Nordalmunoko is
very short but very powerful. When he travels fast
he goes like bounce up and down like rubber ball.
So he now nicknamed Kohorti, meaning bouncing up
and down.

Nordalmunoko, being grown man now, decides to see
more of country. He tells his grandmother he would
like to go up on Sacramento river and visit his two
cousins, Norwanchakas and Keriha. He said, they
are fishing there; they are good fishermen; I surely
will get lots of fish from them. His grandmother said
all right. So she got him net bag and good spear pole
to take along. She fill net bag with some Indian potatoes to give to Norwanchakas and his brother, Keriha,
to eat.

Nordalmunoko starts out, goes up through Buckeye
and through Churntown, northwest through gap down
Sacramento river; comes on a flat. There he crosses
to a house. He puts his net bag down on ground and
knocks. Come in, said someone inside. So he opens
door and walks in. Sit down, said Keriha to Nordalmunoko, my brother is down at the fish-house catching fish.

While Keriha was talking Nordalmunoko was sizing
him up. So Keriha goes down to his brother and tells
him a little man had come to visit them. Norwanchakas told his brother, Keriha, not to bother him for he
is great man, their cousin, Nordalmunoko. Keriha
did not pay any attention to his brother; he went back
up to the house and found Nordalmunoko still there.
He tells Keriha go outside east of house, there you
will find net bag of potatoes; get it and bring in house;
it is not heavy. So Keriha goes out and finds it, but
it was so heavy he could not lift it. He goes back
in house and tells his cousin, Nordalmunoko, he
couldn't lift it; so Nordalmunoko goes out, with Keri-

ha following him. He picks it up with one hand, takes
it in house and puts it down as if it was very light.
After seeing what Nordalmunoko did Keriha goes down
to his brother in salmon house, tells him, that little
man visiting us is very strong fellow.

I told you leave him alone; he is very powerful man,
Norwanchakas says to Keriha. They both go back to
house. When Norwanchakas saw his cousin he says
hello, Cousin. I have been fishing for salmon all
morning but haven't had much luck; I left few down
at the salmon house; you can go down to get them to
take home with you.

So Nordalmunoko goes down to the river, takes his
own spear out of his quiver and in a little while he
got so many fish of all sizes they were piled up on
both shores of the river, and then he goes back up
to the house. Keriha tells him come eat dinner, he
didn't have very much cooked, only what his brother,
Norwanchakas, had caught that forenoon.

Now Nordalmunoko ate up all that was put down to eat
and said, I caught few more fish, left them down there
on both sides of shores. You two had better go down
and get them so we can have some more to eat. I
haven't got enough to eat, yet. So Norwanchakas
and his brother, Keriha, went down to the river.
There they found fish piled up on both sides of the
river so deep they could not gather them all, so they
only took what they could pack on their backs. They
went up to the house and told Nordalmunoko they
could not gather all the fish.

Why, says, Nordalmunoko, I thought you, my cousins, wanted some fish to eat so I caught some for
you. Well, I guess I will go and get some to take
home with me for my grandmother. So Nordalmunoko
takes his net bag, puts in it all the fish lying on both
sides of river and tells them to carry it up so that they
can divide them. The two brothers try to lift up the
net bag, which was only half full, but they could not
lift it; they told Nordalmunoko it was too heavy for
them, they had better divide the fish there.

No, said Nordalmunoko, I take home all to myself.
Goodby, my cousins; good luck to you both. He picked up the net bag with one hand and carried it home
to his grandmother.

So this way they lived for a long time. Then one day
when Nordalmunoko was out hunting, on his way home
he met two very beautiful young women. They said,
hello, you are the man we have heard lots about and
all the people everywhere are talking about you. You
had better come with us; there is going to be a big
time 'way northwest of here. But Nordalmunoko says
to them not now, he had better go and tell his grandmother first before he leaves her. So they all went
to his grandmother's house.

When Nordalmunoko got to the house he said to his
grandmother, you see these two young women? They
have come to take me to big time northwest of here
and I am going with them. So his grandmother said,
my grandson, you are going where the people are mean
people. I will make you a stronger bow and arrow.
So she made him very best bow of yew wood and lots
of stout deer sinew rounded on its back. She made
arrows and used eagle feathers from an eagle he had
killed on way home. His grandmother also got him
nice round iron ore rock to take with him and stout
spear pole.

The two young women stayed with them that night.
Next morning, very early, Nordalmunoko got up, went
to deep hole in creek took bath, came back to the
house for breakfast. When breakfast was over and
Nordalmunoko and his two women friends were ready
to go his grandmother gave him best of red flint knife
and arrow points made of same kind of flint to take
along with him. Being near fall of year his grandmother gave him also some new water oak nuts and
branch grapes. He takes his carrying net bag and
puts them all in his quiver. Then he says goodby to
his grandmother and they start off towards north up
through Buckeye, up Churn creek, through gap called
Nordaseekloi (south teeth gap). These two young
women are leading the way. They cross Sacramento
river at Kennett, follow the river all way up to La-

moine; here they stop. While they were resting the
two young women say to Nordalmunoko, we have not
told you and your grandmother who we are, what our
father and mother are. We are daughters of Grizzly
Bear chief. His people are very strong and mighty
warriors. We have ten big brothers who will entertain you when we get home. Now, could you show
us what you can do to protect yourself? Suppose,
now, someone should attack us; how would you defend us?

They looked at Nordalmunoko and seeing him being
little short man they laughed at him. When he heard
them laugh at him he grabs at one big tall tree, up-
roots it and swings it around in circle several times,
knocking everything over.

The two young women said, we believe you are all
right. You may make a great man yet. We will have
you for our husband when we get back home.

So the two women turn east on Slate creek, up west
hill through gap call Numdapomkaloi (west land gap),
went down east fork Trinity river near where is now
Trinity Farm and Cattle Company below Trinity Center,
cross the Trinity river, go west up Swift creek, up the
mountain north side of Wy-kee-dee-pom (leaning north
place), went south on west side of mountain, came to
west of rocky crags of mountain north of Weaverville.
There Nordalmunoko was led by his two young women
friends right to their father's big earth lodge. In there
Nordalmunoko saw his future father and mother-in-law
and brothers-in-law. The Grizzly Bear people saw
him and sized him up. They said to themselves, what
a little man! What those two young beautiful women
want such fellow like him for? We'll get rid of him
soon! They are all making fun of him, now.

Being toward late in afternoon the Grizzly Bear people
are beginning to come in with the game they killed
during day, and they are told that a visitor had come
from east. We must do something to entertain him,
they said.

That night after supper the Grizzly Bear people made

big bonfire and invited Nordalmunoko come in and join
dance -- scalp dance. So they danced in big circle
around fire. They put little Nordalmunoko inside the
circle close to fire. They danced and danced. Every
now and then they tried to push Nordalmunoko in fire
but he would throw them in instead until Grizzly people got tired, and some got burned. So toward morning they quit dancing, finally. They had wanted him
to get sleepy.

Now after second day old big chief, Grizzly Bear,
tells Nordalmunoko he can marry both of his daughters. I know you can take care of them all right, he
said. I am getting old, now. So Nordalmunoko married both of young women. But his ten brothers did
not like him. And others were jealous of him because
old Grizzly Bear chief had chosen him for his son-in-
law. So that night Grizzly Bear people held a secret
council in their own earth lodge; they decided to have
big sweat dance in big sweat house next day.

Soon as daylight came around Grizzly Bear people
built fire in sweat house; and when it was ready to
go in they called Nordalmunoko to come in and join
them sweat and dance. Nordalmunoko said to them,
no, I cannot sweat; I am not used to it. You go ahead
and sweat; I'll stay out and look on.

One of his brothers-in-law says to him, come on in;
have fun with us. And they forced Nordalmunoko in.
He let them do it, but once he was inside sweat house
he made up his mind to show them what he could do to
them. So he tells Grizzly Bear people to put on some
more firewood on fire, make it more warm, saying it
was not hot enough for him. He stood near the door.

His ten brothers-in-law and all the others pile more
wood on fire, figuring they could easily get out when
it got too hot for them. They thought they could get
by him because they forced him in sweat house so
easily, and they could shut him up in sweat house
after they got out. So they all started to dance sweat
dance, little Nordalmunoko near the door, facing
them. The heat was getting so hot in the sweat house
now some commence to make for door; but Nordal-

munoko push them back and he keeps on dancing and
swinging his red flint dagger at them. Finally he kills
few of them. Some are burned to death, including
some of his brothers-in-law.

Nordalmunoko thought now he'd done enough punish-
ment to them so he opens the sweat house door, goes
out ahead and the others followed. They were very
glad to be out. All went down to river, took bath,
came back to earth lodge, ate their dinner.

In the afternoon the Grizzly Bear people challenge
little Nordalmunoko to a game of football. He told
them, I can't; I don't know how to play the game.
Grizzly Bear people said, we'll show you; it's great
game to play.

There were ten big, strong Grizzly Bear people line
up against him. One of them told him which Grizzly
Bear man was holding down the football with one foot
and to go and kick it hard. So Nordalmunoko kicked
at the football hard and burst it into pieces and broke
the Grizzly Bear man's foot, too. Now Nordalmunoko
said to them, get another football that will stand
kicking hard. I want to play with you now.

The Grizzly Bear people could not find one hard enough
so Nordalmunoko said, I got one football with me we
can use. So he took out the iron ore rock, very
smoothly rounded, laid it down on ground and held
it down with one foot and told the Grizzly Bear men
to kick it hard as they like. So they kicked at it and
broke their toes doing it. Several of them kicked the
ball hard and could not budge it; just hurt themselves
instead. Then the Grizzly Bear men commenced bump-
ing Nordalmunoko but they all got knocked down,
either with broken legs or arms. So day being well
in afternoon they said let's quit. They all went back
to their earth lodge.

After supper all went in big council house and talked
over what they were to do next day. They kept little
Nordalmunoko awake all night, figuring to get him
sleepy next day. But instead of being sleepy he gets
out, goes down to river first and takes his morning

bath and come back to the house ready for Grizzly
Bear men, whatever they are going to do with him.
So after breakfast they decided to have a long dis-
tance shooting that day with little Nordalmunoko.

They took him to a place, a big wide open valley,
and there they stopped. They commenced to shoot
across the valley to eastward. All shot except Nordalmunoko so they told him to shoot but he said, no,
I cannot compete with you fellows; you all got better
bows and arrows than I have. They coaxed him, go
on shoot. What's the matter with you? You must got
cold feet! Go on, they said, trying to shake him up.
But he swung at them, saying, then give me a chance
to get ready. Knocking them down right and left, he
took his bow and arrow and said, all right! Now I
shoot.

They all looked at him very closely, thinking with
bow and arrow like that he won't be able to shoot
part way across the valley.

Little Nordalmunoko commence to put his arrow on
string and pulled on it and let it go. The arrow, after
going little way, started to curve downward but took
a new upward start again on over the valley. It took
on more speed as it went further eastward and started
to go over the mountains. As it did so it turned into
big live eagle and flew clear over the mountain and
lighted on high mountain call Puitelltun, a high mountain peak northwest of Copper City. That's why big
eagles have lived to this day on this mountain.

So Nordalmunoko won long distance shooting. And
Grizzly Bear people decide to leave Nordalmunoko
alone from then on, treating him kindly now because
they couldn't do any harm to him; they are all afraid
of him now.

After the day's shooting they went back to their
houses, ate their supper and went to bed early for
the first time since Nordalmunoko came to Grizzly
Bear people's place.

Next morning they all got up early, went down to

river, took their morning baths, came back to the
house and ate their breakfast. This day the Grizzly
Bear people decide to go out game drive hunt. They
went eastward to big high mountain what is called
now Trinity Alps. When they came to foot of mountain they told Nordalmunoko to go up on mountain.
They pointed to a low gap. They said, go there,
watch for game; shoot at them when we drive them
up to the gap and holler for us when you kill lots of
them.

So Nordalmunoko goes up to the low gap and waits for
the game. But he saw that instead of driving game
up they were starting in burning brush fire. He looked around on both sides of the mountain. He saw
smoke rising all around. So Nordalmunoko goes down
a little way east down hill, starts a forest fire, follows it up mountain side until the other fire comes
to the burned ground. Then he goes down the mountain, comes around other way and meets them. He
says, hello, fellows! How are you all? I did not
see any game so I came around other way. Let's
go home. So they all went home without game.

Next morning as usual they all got up, went down to
the river, took their morning baths, came back to the
house, ate their breakfast. The season now being
toward fall the salmon was running in the river full
run. So they says, let's go salmon fishing. They
went long way down the river, came to big long riffle
chuck full of salmon. Little Nordalmunoko was told
to stay on shore about in the middle of them. They
caught lots of salmon. They went to work and pile
the fish all around him until they could not see him.

Now the day is getting toward afternoon. The Grizzly
Bear people told Nordalmunoko he had better gather all
the fish that was on the shore and take them home.
All right, said Nordalmunoko.

He takes his net bag out of his quiver, puts all the
salmon in the net bag, puts it down and tells them to
go ahead, pack it home. Grizzly Bear men could not
lift it; the whole bunch of them tried but could not
move it so they gave up, saying, it's too heavy; you

go ahead and pack it home.

All right, says Nordalmunoko. He picks it up with
one hand, carries it to the house. Grizzly Bear people says to each other, what kind of man is this fellow? He has strength mightier than all of us or anybody else.

Now winter season is coming on and both his wives
got child, two boys. One day Nordalmunoko got tired
living among Grizzly Bear people. He thought he better punish them a little, first, for fun of it so he cause
to come a heavy snowstorm during night. The night
was chilly and they all went to bed. Next morning
they woke up and saw heavy snowstorm. Some house
doors were nearly closed up. When night came again
snow was so deep outside nobody could go out in it.
It was lucky for them that Nordalmunoko had carried
home all that salmon they had caught. Pretty soon
all the food was gone. Grizzly Bear people are starving.

One morning Nordalmunoko told his father-in-law to
go out and clear snow off the ground in front of his
big earth lodge down to the ground. Finally he came
back to his earth lodge and said, it's all done. Little
Nordalmunoko goes out and starts in dancing. He
danced all day into night; he never stop once. His
father-in-law said to his wife, I believe he is some
man, all right; we wait and see what's he going to do
next.

So late that night Nordalmunoko took out the water
oak nuts and planted them in ground, and also the
wild grapes he had brought along with him. He danced
all night. While he was dancing these acorns and
grapes grew very fast; so when daylight came around
there was big, tall water oak tree growing full of ripe
acorn nuts, and nuts was beginning to fall off; and
grapes was getting ripe, too.

He stopped dancing. He goes in his father-in-law's
earth lodge, tells him to let all starving people go
out get something to eat. So his father-in-law did,
and I tell you they were mighty glad to get it. They

fill themselves up so much that they could not move
around.

Springtime is coming round, now. Snow is all gone
off the ground. So Nordalmunoko decides to go back
home to his grandmother. He say to the Grizzly Bear
people, I am going to leave you people for good. I
will say goodby to you all. Hope you will live good.
I will take my two wives and my two sons with me.

So Nordalmunoko and his new family leaves west of
Trinity Alps, goes back same route they had traveled
before, going north of Wy-kee-dee-pom, down Swift
creek, cross Trinity river near mouth Numdaponkalai
(east fork), down Slate creek to Lamoine, and down
Sacramento river. Cross river at Kennett, down
through Nordaseekalai, past Churntown, through
Buckeye to his grandmother's house, south up flat,
east of East Gap.

His two half-Grizzly Bear children grew up and became a Bear people. So there are little bears all
through this country. They look little alongside of
other common bear, even when they are full grown.
They supposed to be descendants of Nordalmunoko.
Indians never kill those kind of bear, claiming they
are part human being.

This end story. I finish.

Story of Tolchuharas and Old Man Sun

Long, long ago there live lots human people, the
Wintu. The country was valley country, big river
running through it. The people were living on both
sides of the river. They were very peaceable people;
did not go out get wars with other people, just stayed
within their district, never go beyond. So this way
they lived for a long time. Men folks would go out
to get the game which they found was plenty and the
women folk would go out get acorn nuts, manzanita
berries and dig wild potatoes. This way they live
on for a long time. Finally it came to time that the

game in the woods was getting scarce; especially
game like deer, bear, elk, antelope and other big
animals. So now men folk had to go out farther away
from home to find the game which they hunted for
everyday food. The people living on west side of
river was doing the same.

Now all this time the people living on east side of
river never thought of going over on the east ridge
and hunt over other side of ridge. Those on west
side of river went clear over on west side of ridge,
they said, and hunted over there. It seems that
these two mountain ridges run parallel to north and
south, both very high ridges.

In meantime, over east of the east ridge there lived
another people, different from ones on west side of
ridge. This country also had a large river and narrow
valley, the valley on east side of river being broken
country. Their leader, a chief named Saiskeyem-ela
(Old Man Sun), had odd looking body; was shape of
round disk. His head, arms, hands, legs and feet
was like rest of human being.

Now, the people living west of this ridge said to
themselves, let's some of us go over to east side of
ridge and hunt over on that side tomorrow. So next
morning they all got up early, went to river, took
bath, came to house, ate their breakfast and was
ready to go hunting. Those that was going over the
ridge was ten big husky fellows. So, these went.
They were gone all day. Others had all come home
already. They wonder what became of them, night
coming on now and no sign of them yet. Some stayed
up to wait for them, others went to bed. Daylight
coming on, they haven't come home yet.

When daylight comes everybody is up, talking to
each other what became of those hunters. They pick
out twenty men, all big and strong fellows, to go
look for those hunters. The others went north and
south as usual to hunt.

Now it's getting toward late in afternoon. Other hunters are coming in, ones that went north and south, but

ones that went east, over the ridge, has not come back yet, like those day before. This went on for a long time. People are decreasing pretty much, now; they cannot find out what cause them not to come home, at least one, anyhow, to tell.

Now, those on west side of river has come over and join them to look for these lost hunters, as they are called now. They met same fate, never show up to tell what happen to them. This went on for a long time. Finally, all the men were gone. Women folk got to going farther away from home, too, going farther to east, uphill now, for acorn nut, tusu (a plant of the parsnip family), manzanita berries and other things. Finally, they too -- women folk -- disappeared same as men folk had; never come back to tell what happen to them. So, in time, they were all gone, too, except one old woman name Pompokitat (earth lady).

Now Olelbes look down to Saiskeyem-ela. He was very angry. Olelbes say to Himself, I will punish Old Man Sun. I will create man who will be mightier than Old Man Sun.

That day old Pompokitat didn't get many wild potatoes; they were getting scarce, too. She came home, cooked her meal, ate and went to bed. During night old Pompokitat dreamed she came to a large bunch of nice wild potatoes and was digging them but woke up before she dug many of them. Old Pompokitat lay awake long time saying to herself, I wonder what kind of dream I was dreaming.

When morning came Old Pompokitat got up and cook for herself what little wild potatoes she dug day before, ate her breakfast and got ready to go out for some more. As Old Pompokitat was going along, looking for wild potatoes, clover and other roots, it being spring of year, she found just a few here and there. All at once Old Pompokitat saw just ahead of her a nice large bunch of wild potatoes. She went right to it and commenced to dig. Old Pompokitat dug quite a lot so she stopped digging and looked in her carrying basket. It was getting nearly full.

She lifted it and it felt heavy to her. Right there she
thought she had better stop, but she hesitated a little.
She thought, I better dig some more. So she did.
Then she thought she heard a sound way off distant
like some child crying. She stop and listen for a
while. She did not hear it any more so she start to
dig some more. Again she hears some more of child
cry, this time right straight down in front of her where
she was digging. She grab the stem of the wild potato, dug down with the digger and pull up the root.
Then she saw a tiny little boy baby. It was now crying hard. Old Pompokitat said to the little boy, you
are grandchild and I am your grandmother. I will call
you Tolchuharas (one who was dug).

Now old Grandma Pompokitat got sunflower leaves,
wrapped baby with them and took it home, the baby
crying all the time. She went around gathering up
all the different sweet fruit, even sugarpine sugar,
but the baby, Tolchuharas, would not suck it. Finally
Grandmother thought, I better get e'metconmas (snow
plant). So she went and got it. Meantime baby Tolchuharas is crying all time, never stop. Old Grandma
Pompokitat pull off one of blossoms from stem of
e'metconmas, put it to baby's mouth. The baby Tolchuharas grab it with its tiny hands and sucked it
and stopped crying altogether then.

Grandmother now goes to work making baby basket.
She roll Tolchuharas up in finest otter skin and puts
him in the finished basket.

Now it's getting along towards evening. Grandmother
Pompokitat cooked supper for herself, ate it and went
to bed. During the night she dreamed that Olelbes
told her, take child to holy spring which is just little
way north of your earth lodge. It is called sarwol
(place of magic strength). There, bathe baby Tolchuharas, so he will grow big and powerful, have super-
human strength.

When old Grandma Pompokitat woke up she found herself and her grandchild, Tolchuharas, in a large handsome earth lodge which she had never been in before
in all her life. She got up, took her grandchild, walk-

ed out of her earth lodge and went up north of earth lodge. There she came to a nice clear spring. In this holy spring she bathed her grandchild, Tolchuharas, as she was told to do by Olelbes in her dream. Then she went back to the earth lodge with her grandchild. She cook and ate breakfast.

Now child, Tolchuharas, is growing very fast; is now running around, playing outside of earth lodge, getting stronger every day.

One day Tolchuharas says to his grandmother, I saw lots birds outside. Yes, said old grandmother, they are good to eat. I will make you a bow and arrow, my grandson; you can shoot them. So old Grandma Pompokitat made bow and arrow for her grandson, Tolchuharas, and gave it to him. The boy now goes out and shoots and kills lots of birds and brings them in their earth lodge. His grandmother cooks them and they eat them.

Now Tolchuharas is growing very fast; he is now getting into his young manhood and is hunting farther away. Saw lots of bigger game such as deer, bear, elk and antelope. So the grandmother, old Pompokitat, says to her grandson, Tolchuharas, I will make you better bow and arrow, arrows with good flint on them; some with red flint that you can shoot grizzlies with.

So young man, Tolchuharas, is hunting big game now, going farther up in mountains, sometime going north, sometime south, but very seldom far east.

One day his grandmother, pointing toward east, said to her grandson, see yonder east that ridge? You must not go on top there; just hunt north and south of here and this side of ridge east of here. So Tolchuharas hunted every day, now being big and handsome and very powerful.

One day as he was out hunting he thought to himself, I wonder why my grandmother told me not to go up on top of ridge. Tomorrow I am going to try to get up there on top of ridge. He came home with game and

said nothing to his grandmother about what he was
going to do next day.

Next morning he got up early, went down to river,
took bath as usual, came back to earth lodge, ate
breakfast and got ready to go out and hunt. He went
toward east uphill and saw lots of game. He shot
and killed one large elk which he saw close to him
and went back home with it. Tolchuharas done this
three times. Always kill large deer or big bear just
when he was about to get up on top of ridge.

On fourth day Tolchuharas made up his mind he is de-
termined to get up on the ridge this time. So that
night he didn't sleep very much, thinking about it.

Next morning he got up early, went down to river,
took bath, went back to earth lodge, ate his breakfast, got ready to go hunt. On the way up the mountain he saw lots of game but he did not shoot them.
Just before Tolchuharas got up on the ridge he almost
shot one but went up and got on top of ridge. Tolchuharas stop, look down over east side and sat down.
He saw a narrow valley on west side of large river
and on east side of river he saw it was broken country. On west side of river he saw big village. In
center of village Tolchuharas saw a big earth lodge.
He says to himself, that big earth lodge I see must
be some big chief's home.

All this time he has been looking down to the village
he has not seen anybody yet, so he finally made up
his mind to go back home and tell his grandmother,
Pompokitat, what he saw over on other side of ridge.
Day was still early yet. On way back he killed some
deer, got back to his grandmother's house and told
her what he had seen over on other side of east ridge.
Tolchuharas told his grandmother that he had seen a
large village over there and would like to go there,
visit those people, whoever they were.

So old grandmother heard what her grandson, Tolchuharas, told her, that he would go tomorrow. She says
to him, my grandson, I hate to see you leave me but
I guess you may go. First, before you go over there

you must go north of here. There you will find a nice clear spring which is holy water. You must bathe in that water.

So Tolchuharas went to that spring, took bath and went back to their earth lodge. Meantime his grandmother, Pompokitat, went out and got one big mountain lion (panther) for her grandson to take along for his dog, and also made stout bow and fine arrows. Good flint on the arrows, both red and black flint. She made an extra large arrow, very nicely made, and an ol-wan-noos (flint knife). She made a beautiful otter quiver; also a cap of pine squirrel and gopher hide for her grandson to wear on his head. Then she made a war club of hard yew wood and a spear pole of stout fir wood which she call "sky-pole." These, old Grandma Pompokitat put away in one corner of their earth lodge while her grandson was away, bathing in the holy water. When Tolchuharas came back she did not let him know anything about it. Now night has come on; they ate their supper and went to bed.

Next morning, very early, Tolchuharas got up, went to river as usual for bath, went back to earth lodge for breakfast, ate, got ready to make journey. Now old Grandma Pompokitat told her grandson, Tolchuharas, saying, you are not going like you are; you must change your clothes, put on new ones. She went and got new clothes for her grandson to wear. She brought it to him to dress and went back to a corner of earth lodge and got the panther-dog, the nice big otter quiver full of fine arrows, a fine large bow and big stout war club of hard yew wood and spear pole made of nice hard fir wood which she calls "sky-pole." Also cap made of pine squirrel and gopher hide and big war-bonnet trim with nice eagle feathers, reaching down to the waist. His grandmother told him to wear the cap on his head all time; never take it off. She say to him, keep it on your head all the time; it is your magic power which will warn you when danger come to you. Wear it under your war-bonnet all time.

Now Tolchuharas, being ready to travel, bid his

grandmother, old Pompokitat, goodby and went toward eastward. He was just nearing foot of the mountain when he heard his grandmother holler, come back
my grandson, and get me some wood. Wood is all
burnt out! So Tolchuharas went back, gather all the
big logs he could find, made fire for his old grandmother so she could keep warm in her earth lodge and
said, now, Grandmother, I am going. Tolchuharas
was going up the mountain quite a way when he heard
again same call, come back, my grandson, the firewood all gone; get me some more. So he turn back
again. This time he pull up big tree by roots, break
it up into firewood, say goodby to his grandmother
once more and leaves her.

Tolchuharas is getting pretty well up near top of
mountain and again he hears his grandmother calling him back, saying, come back, my grandson, the
firewood is all burned up. Come get me some more
wood. So Tolchuharas once more turn back. On his
way back he is thinking, what am I going to get for
firewood for my grandmother? I have got all sizes
of timber for firewood already and it won't keep a fire
for my grandmother long. Oh, I know what I do. I
will go and dig up lots of wild sunflower roots for
firewood. So Tolchuharas dug up lots of wild sunflower roots, took them to their earth lodge, made
fire again for his grandmother, old Pompokitat. While
he was making a fire she showed him a cap also made
of pine squirrel and gopher hides. She says to him,
I will wear this cap, too, as long as you be away.
This cap will be letting me know how you are getting
along and where you will be all the time. Here, take
some grub with you, enough to last you while you are
away.

So again Tolchuharas says goodby and good luck to
his old grandmother and went away, same direction,
east up hill, taking his panther-dog trailing right behind him. He is now nearing top of the ridge. He
stops and listens back for his grandmother but he
hears no more call so he goes on top of ridge and a
little over and stops just where he stopped day before. He sat down and looked down to the little village for awhile. Pretty soon Tolchuharas saw two

young women come out of the big earth lodge. Both
had water baskets in their hands. One looked up
toward east. But seeing nobody, they both went down
east toward the river to get water.

While those two young women down at the river were
getting water Tolchuharas took out his bow and arrow
that was made bigger than the others. He got up,
took aim and shot toward the door in the front of the
earth lodge and sat down. Just then the two young
women are coming back with their baskets of water.
They saw a nice looking arrow sticking in the ground.
They stopped and put down their baskets of water.
One of the young women grabbed the arrow and pulled
but she could not budge it, so the other young woman
got hold of it and both pulled but could not move it.
They picked up their baskets of water, went in the
earth lodge and told their father, Old Man Sun, that
there was an arrow, very nice looking one, sticking
in ground front of earth lodge and they could not pull
it out of ground.

When Old Man Sun hears this he get up, goes out,
sees the arrow, grabs it and tries to pull out but can't
move it. He pulls on it a couple of times more, then
quits, leaving the arrow still sticking in the ground.
He goes in his earth lodge and says to his two daughters, it must be my son-in-law, Tolchuharas, is coming to visit us soon.

While all this is going on down at Old Man Sun's
village Tolchuharas is not seen by anyone. He keeps
himself invisible all this time. Now he starts to go
down hill towards the village. He comes to foot of
mountain and walks on little ways and meets a large
monster with long sharp teeth, fiery mouth and long
tail coming right at him. Tolchuharas took out his
war club which he kept in his quiver and clubbed the
monster to death. As he gets nearer the village he is
met by more enemies such as rattlesnakes and poison
spiders. Large grizzly bears come on him and his
panther-dog. Tolchuharas swings his war club right
and left on some while his panther-dog bites others
to death and they killed all that was around them.
Then he stopped, looked around and saw lots of hu-

man bones and skeletons lying all over the ground.
He went on to the big earth lodge where he had seen
the two young women and Old Man Sun. He goes to
the door in front, sees his arrow still sticking in the
ground, pulls it out, puts it back in his quiver and
walks to the door and knocks. Old Man Sun inside
says, come in; walk right in; make yourself at home.

So Tolchuharas opens the door and walks in and is
once more met by furious monsters like dragons, rattlesnakes, grizzly bears and poison spiders. But
Tolchuharas and his panther-dog kills them all. Then
he goes and sits down on east side of fire. He looked across the fire and saw Old Man Sun's wife facing
the wall, a very fierce-looking woman. All at once
she looked across to Tolchuharas but his magic spirit
shot fine flints at her eyes and she drops down dead.

Now Old Man Sun gets up and picks up his dead wife
and those that were killed by Tolchuharas and his
panther-dog, takes them out, goes to work and digs
a large pit, throwing them in. Then he gather up the
ones that Tolchuharas and his panther-dog had killed
outside and buries them all. He comes back in his
earth lodge, sits down and tells his two daughters
they had better give Tolchuharas something to eat,
saying he may be very hungry; he may come from long
way. So the two daughters cooked meat for Tolchuharas and gave it to him. He seemed to eat it all
up clean but was really eating his own food his grandmother gave him to take, saying, always eat your own
food. The food that the two young women gave him
was disposed of by his magic spirit cap he wore on
his head.

Now it is coming on night. Old Man Sun is keeping
Tolchuharas up late, wishing him to get sleepy. Old
Man Sun says to him, my son-in-law, we had better
lay down for night and go to sleep; tomorrow we'll
see what we do.

Soon after Tolchuharas had laid down Old Man Sun
says I am going to hang this big flint rock up here
over you; don't be afraid; this is the place I always
hang it up.

Now Tolchuharas lay awake for a long time; finally
all at once he fell asleep. Old Man Sun know Tolchuharas was now sleeping. He pull on a string
which he had attached to string that flint rock was
hung with. Just then the magic spirit cap tell Tolchuharas to roll to one side, quick. He roll just in
time and saved himself from getting hit by flint when
it fell. It struck the ground floor so hard it shook
the earth lodge. Tolchuharas got up, picked up all
the broken pieces of flint and threw them over to Old
Man Sun, saying, the flint you hung up here has fallen down. You had better take and put it away in
safer place. All this time Old Man Sun's two daughters had not talked or looked at Tolchuharas once.

Morning came again. Tolchuharas got up, went down
to river, took his morning bath and came back to earth
lodge for breakfast. They eat breakfast and finish.
All this time Tolchuharas is eating his own food.
Now Old Man Sun say let's have a nice tobacco
smoke before we go into sweat house I got outside.
My body feels tired. I suppose you feel that way,
too. First we'll have a nice smoke.

Old Man Sun fills up his pipe with all the poisonous
stuff he had and gave it to Tolchuharas, saying, my
son-in-law, take good puff. He took it and was
ready to smoke when it was made to vanish by his
magic spirit cap. So Tolchuharas fills his pipe and
gives it to Old Man Sun. He smoked few whiffs and
commenced to cough almost to death. He gives pipe
back to Tolchuharas and says, now I am going to
heat up the sweat house with nice dry manzanita
wood. So Old Man Sun went to work to heat up the
sweat house very hot, then told Tolchuharas to come
and sweat. They went in. It was scorching hot.
They sat there awhile. Then Old Man Sun says it is
getting cooler. I had better put on some more wood.

He had a pile of human bones covered with dry manzanita wood so he puts the bones on the fire. When
they burn they make the smoke too strong to breathe
so Old Man Sun says, I am going out and cool off a
little; you can stay in longer if you like. I'll be back
soon. He goes out, shuts the sweat house door,

rolls a large boulder against it and stops up all the
holes. Meantime Tolchuharas is acting like he got
up, spits down his saliva, saying, you be here and
make noise like I was dying. Then he takes out his
awl, which he carried in his quiver, and digs down
at the bottom of the sweat house, opposite of side
door, and where Old Man Sun is listening to him dying
inside of sweat house. Tolchuharas come up right behind him and says, what are you saying? Old Man
Sun turns and sees Tolchuharas standing behind him.
He says, oh, I was saying I'm afraid for my good
son-in-law. I must open the door quick! I am so
glad to see you are alive. Let's go in the earth lodge
and have something to eat, have a lunch for the day.

That night they didn't eat supper because Old Man
Sun was wondering what kind of a trap he could set
for Tolchuharas to kill him. He had tried all his
schemes and none was successful. Then he thinks
of a plan. Oh, I know, he says to himself. I will
get my son, Supchet, to act like a fish and appear
in my salmon house tomorrow. That will end Tolchuharas' life on this earth. I am more powerful and
mightier than he is.

Next morning, early, Tolchuharas went down to river,
took bath, came back to earth lodge. The food was
cooked and ready for breakfast. They ate and finish
breakfast. Now Old Man Sun says, my son-in-law,
I am going to take you down to my salmon house. You
can fish for salmon. There is spear pole down there
already. Let's go. So they went down to the salmon
house. They sat there for a while. Pretty soon Old
Man Sun says, I am getting tired. I am going back
home; you stay and watch for fish. I will come back
later. He leaves.

As soon as he was out of sight Tolchuharas takes out
his own spear pole and throws other spear pole away.
He sits in the salmon house watching for fish to come
out but has not seen any yet. It is now getting along
in afternoon; he feels tired and drowsy; once he almost fell in the water but his panther-dog grabbed
him and pulled him back.

Now day is well in afternoon and Tolchuharas is very
tired and is thinking he will quit looking for fish and
go back to Old Man Sun's earth lodge but says to
himself I better stay little longer and watch. Pretty
soon he sees a tiny little fish come into the water
in the salmon house. It was down in front of him.
He looked at it for a long time. He says to himself,
it may be the fish I am to spear. So he sets both
his toggles tight on the points and spears right at it
and hits it. The little fish becomes a very large fish
and is now pulling and splashing the water to beat
the band. After a while the salmon house is shaking
down and Tolchuharas is standing on the shore, pulling his spear for dear life. Soon he is pulled into
the river, the water coming up to his knees, now to
his waist, now to his armpits. He calls to his spirit cap and tells the gopher spirit to stop up all the
holes all over the earth. So the gopher spirit went
and stopped up all the holes all over the earth.

Now Tolchuharas begins to pull the large fish out.
He pulls it out on shore and sees he had caught a
very large Supchet. Tolchuharas now takes out his
war club and knocks him on head and kills him. He
carries it back to Old Man Sun's earth lodge, lays
it down on the ground by the door, goes in and says
to Old Man Sun, well, I got the fish. I laid it down
outside; you can go out and get it.

Now it is getting dark and they had not eaten any
supper that night, but Tolchuharas is not very hungry since he eats his own food.

Next morning Tolchuharas got up, went down to river,
took bath, came back to earth lodge. He sees Old
Man Sun is getting ready to go some place. He says
to Tolchuharas, let's go just across the river and play
at springing off from tree. After we get through from
playing we can come back and eat our breakfast. It
is fine place to play. I used to play there when I was
young man.

So they went down to river, eastward, came to a foot-
log, very smooth, Old Man Sun leading the way. He
goes on ahead and stops in middle of foot-log and

tells Tolchuharas to come on. Tolchuharas and his
faithful panther-dog walks on footlog. Just then Old
Man Sun goes on farther ahead and stops near the end
of foot-log. He sees Tolchuharas is about middle of
foot-log so he shakes and rolls it back and forth, but
Tolchuharas and his panther-dog cross over safely.

Now they are heading a little towards east, then due
east. They come to a big tableland. Tolchuharas
sees one tall tree standing in open field. Old Man
Suns says to him, my son-in-law, you see that tall
tree yonder in middle of the field? That tree we are
going to play on. As they went to the tree Tolchuharas saw some human bones laying all over the
ground. Old Man says to him, I'll climb up first.
I'll stop up about middle of tree; you pull the tree
down and let it go.

Tolchuharas did what he was told to do; he pull it
down and let it go. But Old Man Sun had climbed
down on south side of tree and was standing there,
waiting.

Old Man Sun now says to Tolchuharas, now you go
up. Go little higher than I did. It is fine! So Tolchuharas climbed up and stopped just two limbs higher than Old Man Sun had. Old Man Sun pulls tree
down and lets it go. Meantime, while Tolchuharas
was up in tree he pulls his spear pole out of his quiver and slides down on it and he stands, waiting for
Old Man Sun. This went on several times, each taking his turn. Finally, Tolchuharas got up pretty nearly to the top and Old Man Sun thought now he got a
chance to kill him, so he pull the tree way down to
the ground and let it go. The tree snap like a whip
but he found Tolchuharas standing at foot of tree,
waiting for him.

Old Man Sun is showing sign of becoming nervous
and tells Tolchuharas he cannot go up any more. Do,
please, my father-in-law; go up once more, says Tolchuharas. This is first time Tolchuharas ever call
Old Man Sun his father-in-law.

So Old Man Sun climb up once more and it is the last

time. After climbing not so high as Tolchuharas did he stops, saying, this is highest I want to go up.

No, my father-in-law, my good man, go on up where I sat. It is fine view. You can see quite a way around the country. Go on up higher!

Old Man Sun begged not to but finally said he would go up higher. When he got up just one limb higher than Tolchuharas had, his son-in-law talked to his magic spirit cap, saying, make Old Man Sun stay up there this time. He pulled down the tree for the last time, clear down to the ground, and let it go. It swung so swift it made crashing sound and shook the earth all over.

Tolchuharas stood and waited a little while. Finally he heard, 'way up toward the sun, someone hollering down to him, saying, you are mightier man than I am. I will respect you, mighty superhuman man of all men. Throw me up nice white feather cap made of very fine feathers and fire-making wood sticks that will make sun very bright; make sun hot so that people on earth get warm.

All this time Old Man Sun's two daughters knew their father was killed because blood dropped in their hands when Tolchuhars sent him up to sun.

Now Tolchuharas goes back to two daughters, who are only ones left. He says to himself I am going to finish all. I will bring those two young women and swing them to moon where they can stay and light earth at night. So Tolchuharas came to Old Man Sun's former earth lodge, found the two daughters and told them they must follow the fate of their father. He took them to the tall tree, told them to climb up to where their father had sat and face each other.

I am going to swing you onto moon. There you two will stay. Once in a while you will cover your father's face, but not long. So Tolchuharas pulls down on the tree and lets go of it; so those two daughters of Old Man Sun swing up on moon. From there they made the moon shine and give more light at night.

To this day if you look at the moon when it is full
moon and sky is clear you can see two woman's faces,
one on south half of moon looking northward and one
on north half of moon, looking south. One on south
show up plain; it show full forehead, nose, mouth,
chin and neck. One on north shows not so bright; it
show its face: nose, mouth and chin.

So now Tolchuharas is ready to go back to his grandmother, Old Pompokitat. He hurries along. Finally
comes in sight of their earth lodge. He sees lots of
newcomers are living all around their earth lodge.
Old Grandma Pompokitat sees her grandson come in
sight. She cries out, my grandson is coming! She
goes out and meets him and soon everybody is around
him saying, come home, our great hero! Let's give
him a big celebration. So they had war dances and
big feast.

This ends this story. I finish.

Story of Pine Squirrel and his Uncle, Old Badger

Long ago there came to being a Kalamas (pine squirrel)
family, a man and woman. Pretty soon they bear a
child and were increasing very fast and lived for long
time that way. The menfolk would go out hunt for
game for food. They'd kill deer and other game and
womenfolk would go out and gather acorn nuts and
berries and wild potatoes and greens. So this way
they lived for long time.

Pretty soon there came a change; everything was getting scarce and winter was getting colder, food getting
scarcer. So pretty soon some were dying of hunger
and freezing to death. So when springtime came a-
round there were very few left. These lived just south
of Mt. Shasta on Onion creek. Just little east of
Onion creek there still stands a reddish color mound
which they had used for their earth lodge.

Now, of the few was left, some move away and only
ones stayed back were one family of Kalamas and one

old Part-shochet (old badger). These lived for a while and pretty soon Pine Squirrel family began to die off and left only one Pine Squirrel boy and Old Badger. This Old Badger was the Pine Squirrel boy's uncle, so Old Badger took his nephew in his old shabby house.

Old Uncle Badger being old never know how to hunt for deer and other game; he could only gather acorns, wild chestnuts, hazelnuts and berries for food. This way they live, the two of them.

After a while young Pine Squirrel growed up to be young man. He made himself a nice stout bow and arrow. One day he told his old Uncle Badger they had better build them a new house to live in. Old Badger said all right, go ahead. So young Pine Squirrel went to work and build them a nice big house.

Now young Pine Squirrel being full grown, big and handsome young man, he can go out and bring in food for both of them. His old Uncle Badger was very poor, for in his younger days he never did much for himself; he just lived and that's all. So now young Pine Squirrel had to go out and get food and clothing for himself and for his old Uncle Badger.

Now young Pine Squirrel was getting very rich; he had everything he could wear: lots of beads and shells of all kinds and lots of woodpecker heads to wear on belt. They lived this way for long time. Finally one day young Pine Squirrel being lonesome told his old Uncle Badger, I am thinking of going south; I hear some big time there, a hunting big time. I may get wife bring home. You know we are lonesome just living here by ourselves. I am going tomorrow morning and you can stay home till I come back. But the old Uncle Badger said no, I don't want to stay here, I'll go with you. No, you better stay here, Uncle, it's very long ways I am going and I don't think you can make the trip.

Yes, I can, my nephew, said Old Badger. All right, Uncle, be ready tomorrow morning, be ready early.

Now, Old Uncle Badger never got up early any time
before this; he would lay 'most all day in house face
to wall, not even wash his face when he get up for
his meals.

Next morning young Pine Squirrel got up long before
daylight, made fire and was cooking food for breakfast; he saw his old Uncle Badger get up and wash
his face, move around quite lively for old man. Breakfast is ready so old Uncle come and eat. It was still
dark outside. They ate their breakfast and got ready
to go. Old Uncle Badger didn't have much to wear
but his nephew young Pine Squirrel had lots to pick
out to wear. So they start to go south, old Uncle
Badger with his shabby clothes on and young Pine
Squirrel with his fine clothes on. But he took some
ordinary clothes with him which he carried in his
carrying net, but his uncle did not see these.

So they traveled that first day a long way and when
night came they camp. Next day young Pine Squirrel
get up early, cooked food for breakfast, eat their
breakfast and start for south. Young Pine Squirrel
asked his uncle how he felt for trip. Old man said
fine, my nephew. We got long way to travel yet,
Pine Squirrel said, we only just started so let me
know when you get tired and we will rest up a day.

On about tenth day young Pine Squirrel said we are
near the big time place, by tomorrow evening we will
get there. All this time old Uncle Badger is getting
stronger.

Next morning young Pine Squirrel got up early as usual, cooked their food, eat their breakfast, started on
their last day journey. Time being summer, as they
travel farther south it was getting hotter for them,
especially for old Uncle Badger.

It was getting sundown when they got near the big
time place so they stopped. Young Pine Squirrel looked at his old Uncle Badger; he felt sorry for him with
those poor clothes which he wore. So young Pine
Squirrel said, Uncle, you wear my fine clothes, take
off your old clothes, throw them away, they are no

good to you any more. So Pine Squirrel took off his fine clothes and gave them to his old Uncle Badger, including his fine beads and best woodpecker head belt, and his best bow and arrows. Then he tells his old Uncle Badger go ahead, I come in later. I'll wear my ordinary clothes when I come.

So old Uncle Badger goes on ahead. As he is nearing big time place he could see chief making his evening speech just outside his earth lodge. Old Uncle Badger went right straight to earth lodge and went right in. In there he saw two young women. Of course, he did not know whose daughters they were. Anyhow, he went and sat between the two young women.

After a while when chief got through talking he comes in. In the earth lodge he sees a fine and wealthy looking person sitting between his two daughters. The chief order his cooks to give the man who has just come something to eat. So they gave old Uncle Badger best food they had, mind you. Old Uncle Badger didn't look very old, only looked very handsome.

After a while young Pine Squirrel comes in wearing his ordinary clothes, but nobody notice him; they did not even give him anything to eat. Young Pine Squirrel sat for a long time thinking every minute someone would feed him. Finally he saw two children one side by themselves eating some food so he goes over to them and says hello to them and they answers hello to him. Pretty soon the two children gave him some food to eat. Nobody had notice young Pine Squirrel yet, not even the chief. Those two children were orphans but young Pine Squirrel did not know they were. They were living there with the chief. The young Pine Squirrel notice that the chief was not treating those children right; he would hardly talk to them.

Now the chief was making his night speech and also telling his people what to do and where the hunters were to go and hunt.

The old Uncle Badger is now having the best time of his life sitting between two daughters of chief, everybody looking at him because he looks so rich and handsome in his nephew's clothes.

Now night was getting late so the chief says well,
we had all better go to bed for night. Young Pine
Squirrel just laid down where he had sat near those
two children.

Morning came around; everybody is getting up for day.
Some went down the river, take morning bath. Even
old Uncle Badger is going down river for morning bath,
first time in his life. Young Pine Squirrel goes down
to the river later. Nobody notice him yet.

All come back up the earth lodge, ate their breakfast,
got ready to go out to hunt. Old Uncle Badger went
with them, too. He never hunted for deer or any other
game before. His nephew, young Pine Squirrel, saw
him go with them. He wondered what chance he had
getting deer or other game. So now he tells the two
children to move out away and camp with him. He
did not know that they were orphans.

They picked a camp and then went out with him to
gather some pine and hazelnuts. While out gathering nuts, the young Pine Squirrel asked them who
their father and mother were. They said they had no
father or mother; they were both dead, and they had
been living with the chief since their parents died.
They said that the chief had not treated them good,
not even given them enough food to eat, only at night-
time. So young Pine Squirrel felt very sorry for them.

That day they gathered lots of sugarpine nuts and wild
chestnut and hazelnut and took it back to their camp.
On the way young Pine Squirrel killed some nice gray
squirrels. The day was getting toward late afternoon.

Just soon after they got back to their camp the chief's
hunters are coming in, one by one. No game of any
kind with them. Pretty soon they all come in, the
last one, old Uncle Badger. He walked right in earth
lodge and he show the chief, now his father-in-law,
a bloody arrow point and said, I shot at large buck but
I did not hit it hard enough and so this arrow fell off
it. The buck was so big I tracked it long way until I

lost its track.

Now, you see, when in morning all were up in mountain hunting, old Uncle Badger had on his best clothes that his nephew, young Pine Squirrel, had given him day before.

When he went out to hunt with others he walked behind and then laid down and went to sleep and slept until late afternoon. Then he takes one of his arrows, makes his nose bloody and then smears the blood on arrow point, puts it down to dry, lays down and sleeps some more until sundown.

Now, when old Uncle Badger comes in the earth lodge he tells the chief about seeing the big buck and shows him the arrow with the blood on it. So that night the chief said he would go out hunting with him tomorrow. Young Pine Squirrel could hear him from his camp.

That night the young Pine Squirrel wished for the boy and girl to grow fast.

Next morning very early young Pine Squirrel hears the chief make his morning speech. Pretty soon everyone was up, menfolks going down to the river for baths. Young Pine Squirrel gets up, finds his two young friends had grown to be big handsome young man and beautiful young woman. They go down to the river for morning bath, came back, ate their breakfast.

After breakfast the young Pine Squirrel sees his old Uncle Badger now had changed his clothes and was wearing some he had borrowed from someone, and he had left his best clothes that his nephew had lent him to wear. He left his good clothes in the earth lodge with his two beautiful wives, who were the daughters of the chief. So now young Pine Squirrel had a chance to get back his clothes. He is now married to the beautiful young girl. He tells her when all the menfolk go to hunt to go and get his clothes, all the beads, all the red woodpecker heads and belt that his old Uncle Badger had worn. He said, those are my clothes. I lend those things to him. He is my uncle and is very poor. He has nothing; and he never hunt-

ed deer or any other game in his life. I have always
supported him. I feel very sorry for my old Uncle
Badger. I am afraid something may happen to him this
evening when he comes back from hunting.

After telling his young, beautiful wife what to do
young Pine Squirrel said to his brother-in-law, let's
go out and hunt today. So they went to hunt. It was
late, nearly noontime. Pine Squirrel gave his brother-
in-law a nice bow and arrow which he had with him,
they went out to hunt. They hunted about middle of
the afternoon, hadn't seen any deer or any other game
so young Pine Squirrel says to his brother-in-law,
let's hunt back toward camp; we may see one on way
back. Sure enough, after going little ways they saw
two nice big bucks with large horns on them. So they
each shot at them and killed both deers. They skinned
them and, both being very powerful men, they packed
everything with them, putting the deer heads on top of
the load, showing up the horns in plain sight.

The chief, after showing his hunters where to go, he
comes back early and finds out that the young woman
had come and got old Uncle Badger's clothes, beads,
shells and the woodpecker belt, and had told them
that it all belong to her husband, young Pine Squirrel.

When the chief heard it, he was pretty mad. He said,
he has told lie to me, saying he was rich, had lots of
beads, shells and other things.

Late in afternoon young Pine Squirrel and his brother-
in-law comes in with their deers before the chief's
hunters come in. Chief comes out of his earth lodge,
looks over toward young Pine Squirrel's camp and
sees two nice big bucks hung up to tree. After a
while chief's hunters are coming in one by one with
no game. Pretty soon all come in, old Uncle Badger
coming in last, arrow in hand. He shows to chief,
his father-in-law, arrow with blood stains on point
and said, I shot a very large buck, a big fat one,
but I did not hit it hard enough so this arrow fell off.
I tracked it long way until I lost track of it. Maybe
I will do better tomorrow.

When chief heard him say that, he orders his men to throw old Uncle Badger out and beat him up or kill him.

In meantime young Pine Squirrel says to his brother-in-law, let's go and help my old Uncle Badger. I believe they are going to kill him. So they run right over to where they were beating old Uncle Badger and each had bow and arrow in hand, ready to shoot. Young Pine Squirrel hollers to them to stop beating his old Uncle Badger, but chief says no, and orders his men to shoot at them, too. But young Pine Squirrel and his brother-in-law was too quick for them; they shot down several of chief's men. So chief says to them to stop killing his men. Young Pine Squirrel says to chief, not until you give up my old Uncle Badger. Then I will stop.

All right, said chief, you can take your old Uncle Badger to your camp.

So young Pine Squirrel and his brother-in-law picked up and carried old Uncle Badger to their camp. He was almost dead from the beating he got from chief's men. Young Pine Squirrel and his brother-in-law doctored up old Uncle Badger best they could.

Later in evening chief send one of his men to young Pine Squirrel's camp who told him that the chief wants to see him in the morning to make settlement for damages he had done his men. All right, said young Pine Squirrel to the man, go back and tell chief I'll see him tomorrow.

So that night young Pine Squirrel wished that the chief and all his men would go to sleep early and sleep way into noon next day. During the night young Pine Squirrel and his brother-in-law doctored old Uncle Badger until he got good and well. So they left camp in middle of night, going north toward Mt. Shasta. They travel and travel that night. Old Uncle Badger is traveling much faster than when he was traveling south.

Early in morning, just before sunrise, they come to

a nice creek. They stop and cook their breakfast.
After breakfast young Pine Squirrel looks down south,
wishes to cloud up sky and make heavy rainstorm
back of them so that the chief and his men could not
follow them.

Sure enough, it did rain. When the chief and his men
woke up about noon they saw it was storming so hard
they did not follow young Pine Squirrel and his young,
beautiful wife, his brother-in-law and his old Uncle
Badger that day, and never did, after all.

Young Pine Squirrel, his beautiful wife, his brother-
in-law, his old Uncle Badger got back to their home
south of Mt. Shasta, and lived over again.

After living with them one winter and summer, young
Pine Squirrel's brother-in-law says, I am going to get
married soon to a young, beautiful badger woman who
I met yesterday. I will marry her tomorrow. So they
were married next day. They had big time.

Young Pine Squirrel's brother-in-law says, we are going northeast of here to live; that place will be named
Badger place. So to this day a mountain is called Badger mountain.

After a while old Uncle Badger get sick and, being
very old, died.

Young Pine Squirrel now has large family and are living
very happy. Everything fine all 'round.

This ends this story. I finish.

Story of Wineepoko and Supchet

Long, long ago there lived at Flume creek about three
miles below Castella lots of Indians. Some lived in
common houses, some in earth lodges. There was one
man who had twelve sons. The Indian men hunted for
deer and some went fishing for salmon, while the womenfolk gathered berries, potatoes and greens, the

season being summertime. They hunted north, south
and east across the Sacramento river. They killed
plenty game and caught plenty fish, so they always
had plenty to eat.

As the time went by the people were increasing, so
game was getting scarce in those directions where
they had been hunting most; so some went hunting
toward west, following Flume creek.

This one man, Wineepoko, who had twelve sons, was
chief of people and also was bow and arrow maker who
had superhuman strength for a little man, for he was
short in his make-up.

While the other men would go out hunt he and his
twelve sons stay at home making bows and arrows with
good flint points on the arrows. He was teaching his
sons to follow his trade for a living.

Pretty soon his oldest son got married and they lived
by themselves.

One day when they went hunting westward one went
farther west up hill. He saw a large deer 'way west
nearly to the top of mountain and finally caught up
with it and killed it. It happened to be on ridge east
down hill toward Flume creek. While he was skinning
the deer he saw a nice large grouse on a limb of fir
tree near him. Instead of finishing skinning his deer
he goes to shooting at the grouse until he shot all
his arrows away. Still the grouse sat on the limb,
never moved. Just then he looked westward. He
saw a large tall man coming towards him. Nearer he
came. He looked terrible in his face, but he waited
for him, to see who he was. Finally the tall man
comes up to him, says, hello, my good man. What
a nice deer you have killed. Have you shot at my
dear pet grouse? One is sitting there on limb on tree.

Wineepoko's son said, yes, but I could not hit it.

This tall big man that he is talking to is Supchet who
lives west of big rock mountain, west of Castella,
head of south fork of Castella creek. This grouse

that sits on limb of fir tree is a magic grouse put there by Supchet to fool Indian people. So now after talking a while, Supchet says to Wineepoko's son, you look young and strong, what say let's wrestle?

Other fellow say no, but Supchet begged him to wrestle. He caught hold of his arm and told him to come on, get up. But Wineepoko's son said, no, I don't want to wrestle.

Supchet, being much bigger man, pull him up on his feet; then they wrestle and fight for a while until Wineepoko's son gave out. Then Supchet threw him down hard on ground, took his heart out, took it home, going west.

All other men have gone home with their game by now, but this one man has not come home yet. Night coming on and he still hasn't showed up. His father and mother and brothers are getting worried.

Next morning they all got up early, went down to river, took bath, came to the house and ate breakfast. One of Wineepoko's sons says, I will go out and look for my brother while others are hunting for game. All right, said old Wineepoko. The other sons stayed with their father at home making bows and arrows.

After going up westward, the one that is looking for his brother comes to a ridge going west up hill, finds his brother's tracks, follows the track up the ridge. He sees where his brother had sat down to rest. While standing and looking around he saw a nice large grouse sitting on a limb of a fir tree. Not hunting for deer, he thought he had better shoot at grouse, so he shoots at it. He shot and shot until he shot all his arrows away. He looks at the grouse, thinking what a poor shot he was. While looking around he looked towards west and saw a tall man coming toward him. He waited to see who he was and where he came from, for he was total stranger to him. He saw he was very rough looking and ugly.

The tall man comes to Wineepoko's son and says hello, my good man. Where have you come from?

Very far?

It seems Wineepoko's son did not find his brother's body so he ask Supchet if he had seen anybody day before.

No, said Supchet, you are only one I have met so far. So they talked awhile. Finally Supchet says to Wineepoko's son, you seem to be young and strong, what say let's wrestle?

Wineepoko's son said, no, I cannot wrestle; I am not strong enough for that game.

Oh, come on, said Supchet, I show you how.

So he grabs hold of one arm, pulls Wineepoko's son up and grabs him around the waist. They start to wrestle. Finally comes to fighting. They fight and fight until Wineepoko's son gave out and fell to ground. Then Supchet killed him, cut his chest open, took out his heart, took it home to west.

Meantime, like day before, other hunters are already going home with their game. After sunset, and Wineepoko's son has not come home yet. Finally night comes on. He has not showed up. Now all the people are worried and say to old Wineepoko, let's go in your big earth lodge, hold meeting what to do. So they all went into the earth lodge, menfolk only, and decide old Wineepoko and his ten remaining sons go look for his two lost sons, one son every day until all ten sons not come; then old Wineepoko, the father, go last.

All agreed. So every day these ten remaining sons go out to look for their brothers. Each day no one come home to tell their father and mother where they been. Finally, all the sons were gone.

When the last son, who was the oldest, was gone, old Wineepoko calls the rest of his people to come in his big earth lodge and hold another meeting. Old Wineepoko told his people he would go out look for his lost sons and if he did not come home for them all to look for him next day. All agreed.

Old Wineepoko, for first time, got up earlier than
others. He went down to river, took bath, come back
to his big earth lodge, ate his breakfast. Then he
gather up all the tools he use for making bows and
arrows and put them in his best otter quiver. Also
took his smoking pipe and strongest tobacco he had,
He says to his wife and all his people, I am going.
If I don't come back tonight all you men look for me
together. Not few; all of you, mind you.

So old Wineepoko went west, up Flume creek, came
to ridge leading up west. He saw his lost sons' footprints. When he saw those tracks he commence to
sing "Wini, wini, wini, wini," his mournful song as
he went along. He kept up his singing until he saw
a nice large grouse sitting on fir limb just ahead of
him. When he got near the tree he stopped and looked at it a while. Finally he thought he had better
shoot at it. So old Wineepoko got his bow and arrow
out of his quiver and shot at the grouse. He only
knocked the feathers off of it. The grouse flew a-
way. It was the first time it ever got touched by anybody.

Old Wineepoko sat down on a rock and looked around.
He found that he was sitting where someone had been
fighting. He saw the ground was pretty well worn
down. While sitting there singing his mournful song
he looked to the west and saw a tall man coming toward him. He came slowly, taking his time.

Old Wineepoko, looking at him all time never takes
his eyes off of him; he saw he was very mean looking
and ugly. The tall man comes to him and says, hello,
old man. Are you taking rest here? You found good
place to rest.

This was Supchet, a giant. Instead of answering him
old Wineepoko sings his mournful song, "Wini, wini,
wini, wini."

Supchet says, I am talking to you; answer me. Where
have you come from? Tell me, quick.

Old Wineepoko kept on singing, "Wini, wini, wini, wini."

Don't "wini, wini" me. Come, old man, talk to me like man, says Supchet.

Old Wineepoko stopped and looked at him sharp and said, when you get old and feeble as I am you'll talk to your chiefs.

Supchet says, old man, fill your pipe with tobacco. Let's smoke.

Old Wineepoko said, when you get old and feeble as I am you'll fill your pipe and give it to your chiefs to smoke.

Finally Supchet said, I'll fill my pipe. We'll have a smoke. So he filled his pipe with poison tobacco, lighted it, and handed it to old Wineepoko. He got hold of it but the pipe fell to the ground and got broken.

Supchet said, now you have broken my pipe! What you do that for? He was gettting angry now.

It did not like my hand so it broke, old Wineepoko said.

Supchet said, now you fill your pipe with your tobacco. Let's smoke yours.

So old Wineepoko filled his pipe with strongest tobacco he had, lighted it, took couple puffs and handed it to Supchet. He smoked. After three or four puffs he choked. He almost fainted. He threw pipe down on top of rock, hard as he could, but it did not break. Supchet said to old Wineepoko, your tobacco is no good; it pretty near choke me. What kind of tobacco is it?

It is good tobacco. Finest I got, old Wineepoko said.

After sitting down a while Supchet said, let's wrestle, old man.

Old Wineepoko said, when you get old and feeble as
I am you will wrestle with your chiefs.

Oh, come on, old man. Supchet was getting desperate
now. Come on, I said, old man, come on! He gets
hold of one of Wineepoko's arms and pulls him up;
being young and big and powerful, he pulls him up
on his feet.

Now you grab me 'round my waist, Supchet says to
him.

I can't, says the old man, I'll grab hold here. And
he grabs around Supchet's legs.

No, no, old man, up higher. He takes hold of old
Wineepoko's arms and puts them around his waist.

All right, says old Wineepoko. He squeezed Supchet
hard. They fought for a long time. Finally old man
was getting tired. He tells his tools that he had sack-
ed in his net bag to come out and help fight this man.
So all the tools jumped out of net bag, went to pound
and drill into Supchet's legs and finally got Supchet
begging for mercy. But old Wineepoko would not listen
to him; he finally knock him down and kill him.

Old Wineepoko now takes out his flint dagger, cuts
Supchet's chest wide open and takes his heart out.
He also cut scalp off Supchet's head and ties both
on a stick. He goes west, following trail where
Supchet came. He got to Supchet's earth lodge,
found Supchet's wife and daughter, killed them both,
cut out their hearts and scalped them and tied them
on stick with Supchet's heart. He looked around in
the earth lodge. He saw twelve hearts hung up,
pretty well up in the earth lodge. It was his twelve
lost sons' hearts. He takes them down, goes back
to his home. On way he comes to a lake; here he
washes his twelve sons' hearts, making them look
fresh. He goes on down east and the day was getting pretty much in afternoon.

Just before he got to his earth lodge he leaves his
sons' hearts in a deep hole in Flume creek, then goes

on to his earth lodge.

His wife and all the other people were glad to see him
home. They saw he had killed the Supchet; he had
three hearts and three scalps tied on a stick.

That night they dance war and scalp dance. About
toward daylight all twelve Wineepoko's sons comes
home alive.

So this ends this story. I finish.

Story of Sedit, the Coyote and Torraharsh, the Sandhill Crane*

Long, long ago there lived a family of Sedit and Torraharsh, the coyote and the sandhill crane, at Wy-ken-
pom-charrow (Shasta Valley).

For a long time they lived close together, roam all
around all over the valley and hill, the two always
together, the Sedit and Torraharsh.

One day Sedit asked Torraharsh, saying, "My nephew"
(as a rule Sedit is 'uncle' to all being), "let's travel
to some other places; we have been born and have
grown up together right here and stayed too long one
place; let's go places where we can see some other
peoples; we may learn something new, find out what
is going on other places, then we can come back and
tell folk back here at home."

At first the Torraharsh didn't like the idea and said,
"No, Uncle Sedit, I am not much of a traveler so I
can't go with you. Maybe some other time we can
go."

---

*This legend was written by Grant for publication in the yearbook of
the Siskiyou County Historical society, The Siskiyou Pioneer (Yreka,
California, August, 1947), pages 21-22, 35-39.

So Sedit and Torraharsh talked it over so much, before they knew what time of year it was, it was coming around fall of year. As a rule Sedit wants to do
lots of things and see things and satisfy himself,
no matter what it may be. So Torraharsh said, "All
right, Uncle Sedit, I will travel with you. Where
shall we go first, Uncle Sedit?"

He said, "You see those two high mountains south
of here? We go south between those two high mountains."

So each went to their parent's home to tell them what
they decided to do. Sedit and Torraharsh being both
young, they thought they should be well dressed with
beads and clothing and of course good bow and arrow
with nice flint points on them. Each of their parents
gave them both good advice not to get in trouble with
anyone; always try to be good and friendly with everybody. So they were well dressed and was given each
good many things to take along with them.

So now they start on their way down south to visit
strange country for the first time in their young manhood. They travel southward to the divide between
those two high mountains. Finally they got up on
divide and they stopped and looked around and looked west to the high mountain. Sedit, the coyote,
said, "I believe that mountain is called Num-mel-
be-le-sas-pom" (Mt. Eddy). "I have heard talked
about back home." And Sedit looked toward east and,
pointing, said, "My nephew Torraharsh, I believe that
mountain is called Bohem Puyuik." (Meaning high
peak: Mt. Shasta).

They stopped a while and looked down south and
southeast and southwest. After a while they walk
down a ways and came to a valley. After going little
farther south they came to a village and saw lots of
people, first time since they left their homes. Of
course Sedit all the time is to do the talking and his
nephew, Torraharsh, just to listen. So Sedit ask
these people what was this valley called and they
told him it is named Wy-num-charrow (meaning northwest valley, now Strawberry Valley). And told them,

"There is bigger valley down south; I suppose there you two are going."

Sedit says, "Yes, my nephews and nieces, my nephew and me here are going down that way."

The people ask the Sedit and Torraharsh if they knew the road where they heading for. Sedit said, "No, we don't so we would like to know which road is best to go down.

The people told them to follow straight on down the road they are on until they came to river called Num-tce-pom-all-way-nem (Sacramento river). So Sedit said, "We are glad you told us what road to follow."

They travel on down until they came to a flat ground. Here they came on to a village again and they stopped and talked to the people they met. Sedit says to them, "Glad to see you, my nephews and nieces. Me and my nephew here are going down south. Which road are we supposed to travel. And what is this place called?"

So the people told Sedit it was called No-way-nes-pom (meaning looking down south; place is just north of Shasta Springs). From this point looking down south Sedit says to Torraharsh, "My nephew, you see that big high mountain down south? We will go down that way." So they travel on down a ways and came to river, Num-tee-pom-all-way-nem (Sacramento river) at Wy-yel-cho-po-sas (meaning sound of an animal walking upstream; at Upper Soda Springs, a flat in north Dunsmuir where State highway 99 crosses the river now). Here again they came to many peoples. It being late in day the Sedit says to Torra-harsh, "My nephew, let's stay here overnight."

That night Sedit, as he always do, asked the people what trail to follow. "We are going down south to see different country and different people." So the good people told them to cross the river right here and follow the trail on west side of this river far as you want to travel down south.

Next morning they got up early, ate their food they
had carried with them and said to the people they are
on their way down south, hoping to see some of the
country as they go down farther.

Sedit says now to Torraharsh, "My nephew, let's
make long travel today."

They travel on down the Num-tee-pom-all-way-nem
all day until they came to place called Wy-te-num-
mal (meaning northwest up). Here they come on to
lots of people. Sedit says to Torraharsh, "My nephew, the ground is changing very much. I believe we
are going to see better land ahead of us before long."

So they stayed all night and got up early next morning,
ate their food and was ready for travel down south.
Sedit asked the people how much more farther down
they are going to go before they see the big valley
they supposed to see. The people told them they
got a long ways down to go yet. So Sedit and Torraharsh starts on their way down south.

They came to a valley called Wy-te-charrow (meaning
north valley). They went on down. They cross a big
creek called Kor-so-num-wakit (meaning west lung
creek; Dony creek); went on down through flat and
cross another big creek called Up-pam-way-yal-ko-
harm-mes (meaning north up falling); went on down
until they came to a little flat. There they stopped
and Sedit looked around again and said to Torraharsh,
"My nephew, the country is changing again. The
mountains on the east and south are getting lower.
Now we go on down and see some more."

They cross another big creek called Up-num-wakit
(meaning elderberry west creek: Sugar Loaf creek).
Here, after crossing the creek, Sedit stopped and
said to Torraharsh, "My nephew Torraharsh, let's
walk faster and cover more ground; we may get down
to where we figure to be quicker. I very much like
to see the people there. I expect we will see lots
of them." So now they travel faster, Sedit leading
and Torraharsh following behind.

Before they knew it they came to a big creek again called Pa-sa-way-wakit (meaning cliff north creek: Backbone creek). This time Sedit didn't stop, just went on, always in lead. Finally they came to a place called Bar-ras (meaning eating place). Here they saw lots of people catching many fish of all kinds. (This place is at old Coram smelter, just little south of old Kennett dam, now under Shasta lake). Here they stop for a short time. Sedit asked the people how much farther south they got to go down to see the big valley.

The people asked them to stay and have something to eat. They told them they got only little ways to go, but Sedit so anxious to see this big valley and the people down there he said, "No, we can't, we better be going."

So they travel on south, Sedit leading as usual, telling Torraharsh, "My nephew, let's travel little faster."

They came to a creek called Waith-col-wakit (meaning salt mouth creek). Here they come on to some more people. They see them catching some fish. Sedit asked the people, "Are we near the big valley?" The people told them, "Yes, you are near there. You look east from here, you are seeing northern end of the big valley you are looking for, and just east of here there's lots of people. They have a big earth lodge and are having big time." Here they stopped and looked around a little. They saw the country much more flat, especially looking north, east and south. They see no more high mountains in those directions, except looking west they see big mountain peak called Bohem-bolly (meaning big mountain or high peak: Mt. Bally, just west of Redding).

So now Sedit say to Torraharsh, "My nephew, let's go to see those people and their big times; see what they are doing."

They walk on toward southeast, come to a big flat or valley. From here they traveled a big, wide trail go-

ing straight east. Sedit is very anxious get to that
big time so he tells Torraharsh, "Let's go faster."
So they did.

As they neared the big time they could hear the people talk and holler. Still nearer they went they hear
them singing a grass game song. Sedit says to Torraharsh, "Nephew, we are going to see lots of gambling
while we are here."

The people were very busy looking on the grass game.
They didn't notice that Sedit and Torraharsh were with
them until one side won the game. Then they stopped,
looked around, saw them standing near by. The people said to them, "Hello, my friends. Where have
you come from?"

They noticed that Sedit and Torraharsh had good clothes
and plenty good beads on them and carried good bow
and arrows, very good flint points on it, and carried
bag each on their backs but the people couldn't see
what was in them.

Sedit and Torraharsh talked to the people while they
stopped playing the grass game. Sedit as usual is
doing most of the talking. He tell them, "Me and my
nephew here have come from way up north. We have
heard lots of this country down here. We hear of big
valley and large river, plenty big fish. What is this
place called? We like to know."

So the people told them, "This place is called Nal-te-
pui-dal (meaning southeast place: Redding).

After talking with Sedit and Torraharsh for a while
the people start up betting for another game. The
people seeing these two strangers having good clothes
on them, one of the people challenge them to bet their
clothes. The people put down their beads.

So Sedit and Torraharsh took out their beads from their
bag of beads in place of their clothes.

The people wanted to see their new visitors play so
Sedit and Torraharsh started to deal, using two sticks,

(called poik), one being marked and one blank. Sedit
says to the people, "This is first time me and my
nephew here are going to play." So Sedit and Torraharsh starts in dealing and other side starts to guess
them. They missed them several times and before the
people know, Sedit and Torraharsh wins the game.
So the people starts to bet some more for another
game. This time the people deal and Sedit and Torraharsh does the guessing. This time Sedit and Torraharsh are only two on one side, have no partners like
the first game; they are all playing against them.

Sedit and Torraharsh wins this game so now they are
supplied with lots of extra bets. Now they can play
against any odds.

It is now going into night, their first night at this
place, Nal-te-pui-dal. They played on all through
the night and just before sunrise Sedit and Torraharsh
has won ten straight games, other side none.

They stop playing for breakfast. Sedit and Torraharsh
goes down to the river and takes their morning baths.
Comes back for their first meal at Nal-te-pui-dal.

After breakfast the people sent out runner to tell some
more people to come help them play against Sedit and
Torraharsh. So they came and played against them
for ten straight days and not win single game.

Sedit says, "Torraharsh, my nephew, let us have them
build an earth lodge for us; we got lots of things we
won and it is getting toward winter time. We can pay
them with some of our winnings."

So the people went to work and built them a large earth
lodge. When it was finished Sedit and Torraharsh
move in. Sedit says, "My nephew, now they can
come and play with us all they want to; we have our
own place here now."

It now getting into wintertime, beginning to storm,
and people can do nothing but be in house all time;
only work they can do is to gamble these two strangers all through winter.

Now Sedit and Torraharsh got all the people broke,
winning everything they had. They won from everybody all over the country so they all stopped gambling
for a while, but they didn't wait very long. Two short
heavy-built people comes along. They were pretty
well supply with goods. They talk to the people.
These two people were Yee-laith-tha-ba-nu-po-ret
(meaning gopher brothers).

So Yee-laith-tha-ba-nu-po-ret says to the people,
"we heard you are having big time around here. Is
true?" "Yes," says the people, "you see that earth
lodge there?" (pointing to one newly built earth
lodge). "In there are two gamblers. They have won
from us about everything we had. They live in that
earth lodge. That's their gambling earth lodge."

So the people told the gopher brothers to have something to eat. After they got through eating the gopher
brothers said to the people, "Lead us to this two
gamblers' earth lodge. We like to see them very
much."

So the people took them to the earth lodge of Sedit
and Torraharsh and introduced them, saying, "This
is Yee-laith-tha-ba-nu-po-ret. They have come to
see you."

Sedit says, "I suppose you two are here to gamble.
We can now start in, play a grass game."

So they started in. The gopher brothers put down their
bets and the people put down their bets, what little
they had left to bet. The people told the gopher brothers to go ahead and deal, saying, "We have no luck
against them."

It being toward evening. The winter is about half
over. They played that first game, Sedit doing the
guessing. He missed two times and third time he
guesses them both and now Sedit and Torraharsh start
in to deal, with the gopher brothers doing the guessing. They also missed them twice and third time
guessing them. So now the real gambling is going
on. They played a very hard game. Finally Sedit and

Torraharsh won the first game against the gopher brothers, Yee-laith-tha-ba-nu-po-ret. So again the gopher brothers and the people puts down some more bets. Being losing the first game, the gopher brothers takes the first deal. As a rule, always loser takes the first deal when the game begins again.

This time the game didn't last long as first one. The gopher brothers won their first game against Sedit and Torraharsh. And now they put down their bets and the gopher people and the gopher brothers covers the bets. Sedit and Torraharsh starts to deal first. Other side, guessing, missed them twice and third guess caught them both. Other side deals and it wasn't long before the people and the gopher brothers wins again. Now the people are all very glad that they got some of their goods back again and say, "We can now play you two long as you want to play."

As the gambling goes on Sedit and Torraharsh has lost every game since that first game they won against the gopher brothers at the start of the gambling. Being losing everything they had now, they only got the big new earth lodge left, one that the people built for them when they cleaned them up in gambling before Yee-laith-tha-ba-nu-po-ret came along.

Now Sedit says to Torraharsh, "What we do, we'll bet them all they got against our eyes."

Torraharsh didn't like the idea but after a while he says to Sedit, "All right, my uncle, let's do it." So Sedit says to gopher brothers and the people, "We will bet you our eyes against all you got on place! The gopher brothers and people says all right.

Sedit whispers to Torraharsh, "My nephew, you watch them close when they starts to deal" (meaning when they have the two bones, one of them the ace, in their hands).

Sedit and Torraharsh, watching very sharp, did not win this game as they have been before. At last toward the end of game, Sedit and Torraharsh having only one stick left to guess with, Sedit noticed how

gopher brothers had been playing against them; why
they been losing all the time. So Sedit whispers to
Torraharsh, "My nephew, you guess north side and
I'll watch very sharp what they do." So Torraharsh
guess north side for hand holding ace, only having
one stick to guess with, mind you, and if they miss
they figure to lose their eyes.

Torraharsh guessed Yee-laith-tha-ba-nu-po-ret, the
gopher brothers, all right, but Sedit and Torraharsh
both saw another gopher in the ground underneath
where the two gopher brothers was setting, passing
them another bone, or ace, so they could win! That
was the way they were beating Sedit and Torraharsh!

Sedit jumped up, told them they have lost their bet
by cheating! But the people and the gopher brothers
won't give up. They told Sedit and Torraharsh they
have lost the game and better give up their eyes,
both of them!

Being too many against Sedit and Torraharsh, they
grab them, took their eyes out of their heads.

Now Sedit and Torraharsh are in bad shape, being
both of them eyeless. They didn't know what to do!
They both now think of their parents and home up
north.

Sedit says to Torraharsh, "My nephew, we have seen
and done all we wanted but we did not figure we was
to be in shape like we are in now."

Being in springtime, it was nice and warm. Some of
the people took pity on the poor fellows. They load
them up with some grub to eat on their way back home.

Sedit and Torraharsh hold each other's hands when
they started. At first it was hard for them keep in
trail. When they knew they came to a creek they
stopped and waited a while if they could hear anybody or anything around. Pretty soon Torraharsh hears
some kind of noise close to them, but they both sat
very quiet. They can hear a water running near by.
And again Torraharsh hears a noise. It sounded to

him like it was a fish swimming around.

Sedit hasn't heard anything yet because he is so
downhearted he seems to have no memory.

Again Torraharsh hears some more noise very close
by. He holds Sedit with one hand and puts his other
hand into the water. He touches something! He grabs
quick as he could and brings it out of the water. It
was a fish!

At first he didn't know what kind because he couldn't
see it. He felt 'round its head, touched one of its
eyes, pull it out, throw it into his eye socket. Now
Torraharsh can see out with one eye in his head. So
he lets his other hand free from Sedit, takes out other
eye from the fish, puts it in his other eye socket.
Now can see good with two eyes just like he did with
his own eyes before.

Torraharsh hasn't said anything to Sedit yet; but Sedit
thinks there must be something going on and says to
Torraharsh, "My nephew, you must be finding something good. You have let go of me and you are still
standing near to me. Tell me, quick. What is it?
I like to know."

So Torraharsh told Sedit, "When we left up home we
promise we will stick together. Now, we will do
that." So Torraharsh goes to work and catches another
fish, because he see with two eyes now. He takes
out one eye from fish, puts it in Sedit's eye socket.
Sedit could see with one eye good so says to Torraharsh, "My nephew, take out that other eye and put
it in my other eye socket. Quick! I can't wait long."

So Torraharsh take out the other eye from fish and
puts it in Sedit's other eye socket. Now both can see
good with new pair eyes.

They looked around a while and looked at each other,
seeing they had same clothes on that day when they
left their home, year before. They looked at the grub
they were given by the people at Nal-te-pui-dal to eat
on their way back home. They pick it up, throw it

into creek, and Sedit says to Torraharsh, "My nephew, let us not stop and talk to anyone on our way home; we just keep traveling on."

So Sedit and Torraharsh went back home to their parents to live and to raise their own families, telling each other, "Let us not forget those two Yee-laith-tha-ba-nu-po-ret. We get even on them some day!"

And it is so. Right to this day the coyote (Sedit) and the sandhill crane (Torraharsh) hates gophers. They will go out and hunt gophers all day long. By doing it, they supposed to be getting even on them for the crooked gambling they done to them.

Now, I quit.

NOTE:

The following five legends were dictated to my husband's mother, the late Elda A. Masson, when Grant
was a young man living at Upper Soda Springs. The
manuscripts of these stories were found tucked away
in an attic after Mrs. Masson's death and it is im-
possible now to know how much or in what way she
modified the legends in the process of transcribing
them. Presumably she made no changes at all in the
sequence of the narrative, but it is obvious that she
corrected and polished up Grant's English consider-
ably.

Mrs. Masson enjoyed reading James Fenimore Cooper's
Leatherstocking novels, deriving as much amusement from his florid literary style as pleasure from
the narrative itself. Consequently, the reader of
these legends may find, occasionally, phraseology
reminiscent of Cooper. Those of us who knew Mrs.
Masson and appreciated her delightful sense of hu-
mor will recognize in them certain turns of phrase-
her manner of slyly poking fun at Cooper's style.

In the last story, however, "The Lake of the Bleeding Heart,"Mrs. Masson seems to have attempted
to follow Grant's oral rendering of the legend as
closely as possible. One notes a great disparity
between the English used by Grant in the stories he
wrote himself and the English of the "Bleeding Heart"
legend, a difference which may be explained by the
fact that through the years of constant contact with
English Grant in his maturity naturally was able to
write it more correctly than he spoke it as a youth.

The second of these five legends, "Sedit the Coyote
and Torraharsh, the Crane," is a different version of
the longer legend of a similar title which appears earlier in this text and was written by Grant in 1947, as
noted. The version which follows was told to Mrs.
Elda Masson many years previous to that date.

Sedit and Kobalis

In the old days all the animals were persons and Sedit, the coyote, was uncle to everyone except Saiskeyemela, the sun. He lived in the neighborhood of Stillwater with his two sons and was a great trapper of gophers, which he always killed by kicking them to death.

One day in the month called Kilchus (March, beginning of spring) when the grass was growing fresh and the gophers were coming out to eat it, Sedit and his two sons went out to trap gophers along the foothills. They had trapped a great number and had come to the last trap set when they saw someone coming toward them from the south. This was Kobalis, who had gone south in the fall to gamble.

Sedit had seen him there as he passed and had great curiousity to find out all about him.

When Kobalis came up to him Sedit asked, "Where are you going?"

"I am going up north a long way, "Kobalis answered.

Sedit said, "I will go with you." Then he turned around to his sons and said, "Sons, I will leave you here to trap gophers as I have shown you, and when you catch them you must always kick them to death. You must do all things as I have told you, and I will soon come safely back from this trip."

The young coyotes whimpered a little. "Father, we are afraid to stay here alone. What shall we do if anything happens to you?"

Sedit told them that they must always try to keep watch of his progress in traveling, so that they need not worry, and he would come back safely.

So Sedit and Kobalis started on their journey up the Sacramento River canyon, Num-te-pom-ken-wini-mum. Sedit had his gopher trap and, as they went along,

he caught and kicked many gophers. When night came
and they had camped, he cooked them for his supper.
Kobalis neither ate nor drank, although Sedit watched
him closely. They camped at Wagon Valley, west side
of Black Butte.

At last they came out into Wy-ken-pom-charrow (Shasta Valley) and Sedit saw many bands of elk and antelope. He said to Kobalis, "Let me go and hunt these
animals; we need food and their meat would be good
to take along on the journey."

"No," said Kobalis, "we have no time to spare. We
must hurry on our way." And he would not let Sedit
go hunting.

As they traveled, the same thing was repeated: Sedit
hungered for all the game that he saw, but Kobalis
kept him hurrying forward. They camped this side of
Klamath River and Sedit cooked supper for himself.
He watched Kobalis but never could see him eat or
drink. Sedit felt very weary but he held out and tried
to make Kobalis believe he was still active, and ran
around and caught many gophers. But as they went
the gophers grew scarcer.

Next day they went westward, down the south bank
of the Klamath River. After a time they crossed to the
north bank and Sedit could catch no more gophers on
that side, and when they camped he was very hungry
and tired. In the morning Sedit could hardly travel
and he fell far behind Kobalis as they went on. He
could find no gophers or anything else to eat and Kobalis had often to stop and wait for him to come up.
At last he grew so weary that he said to Kobalis, "I
can go no farther. I don't feel good. I think I am
going to die!"

"Well," said Kobalis, "come along the best you can.
Do you see that high mountain ahead of us? We must
cross that and then the end of our journey is near."

Sedit looked at the mountain and he said, "Oh, no!
I can never reach it! I am going to die here! Yet,
I will try, for I am very anxious to see your country."

So they went on, Sedit growing weaker and weaker and
weaker. At last the young man said to him, "Do you
want to eat?" "Oh, yes, yes!" said Sedit, "I am dying of hunger."

Kobalis turned his back to him and took from his quiver
yee-wit (acorn soup) in a small, very small basket,
and dy-ee (dried salmon), also in a small basket, and
Sedit ate and drank 'til he could eat no more. But,
though the baskets were so small and Sedit tried his
best to empty them, yet there was always something
left, and it was the same with the water which Kobalis
gave him in a tiny cup: he could never drink the cup
dry. And they went on again and Sedit was strong for
a time. But when they reached the foot of the ridge,
he was exhausted again. He tried to climb the mountain but soon his strength gave out and he fell down.

"What's the matter?" said Kobalis. "Can't you climb?
I think I shall have to carry you on my back to the
top."

"Oh, yes," said Sedit, "please carry me. I must see
your country and I cannot climb this ridge."

So Kobalis took Sedit on his back and bound him with
his belt so that he should not fall off. And as they
went Kobalis whispered to the Wy-hau-a-koh-ee
(North Wind) so that Sedit did not hear it, and the
North Wind blew gently at first and Kobalis said to
the coyote, "How do you like that?" Sedit answered,
"Ah! That is just what I needed, a fresh breeze to
revive me. That is why I was exhausted down below
there, because there was no air stirring."

As they went on up the wind blew stronger and stronger
and Sedit began to complain of the cold and his fur
began to blow off in little tufts. The wind still blew
more fierce and all his fur was blown off and he was
naked and howling with the cold. Stronger yet the
wind blew and suddenly Sedit's head blew off and
went spinning up into the sky. Kobalis could hear
it talking all the time, "Now I am gone! I am dead
now," until it was lost in the heavens. The wind
still blew and away went an arm into the sky and then

another arm and his two legs, one after the other. But
the trunk still held because of the belt keeping it fast.
Then suddenly there came a stronger gust of wind,
stronger than any that had blown yet, and away went
Sedit's body, whirling up to the high heavens. And
Kobalis went on his way until he came to his home.

But this is not the last of Sedit, the coyote, for I will
tell you how he came to life again and married one of
Kobalis' people and how he left his wife and went toward his own country and fell in with the sandhill
cranes.

Sedit, the Coyote and Torraharsh, the Crane

One day two girls went out into the woods to hunt lily
roots. They went some distance from home and, while
hunting, they came on two dead bodies; one, as if it
had been dead but a few days and the other, as if it
had been dead a long time. They went home and told
their parents what they had seen in the woods. "One
of the bodies was as one of our own people," they
said, "but the other was a stranger. We know not
what tribe."

The old people talked and wondered about it. Who
could have been killed, and why? "None of our own
are missing," said the old man. "There was one
young man who went away a long time ago and I do
not know where he is. But he was only one and you
say there are two dead men there. Tomorrow we will
get the people and go and see them and bury the bodies."

Now, before I go further I will explain to you that
these bodies were those of Sedit and Kobalis, and this
was one of their transformations, for what purpose
is not known. Sedit, the coyote, has great magic
powers and is very curious and must know everything
which goes on and always takes the lead in conversa-
tion. He is also a great gambler and is usually very
lucky.

So darkness came on and this Sedit and Kobalis rose
up alive in the form of two handsome young men and
went into the house of the old people and lay down,
each beside one of the girls.

In the morning they were all much surprised to see
the two handsome young strangers and asked them
where they came from. Sedit answered that they came
from far south. After a little he claimed the older
girl in marriage and Kobalis married the younger.

Sedit grew tired of living there after a while and told
Kobalis that he was going back to his own country
and would fool his wife and leave her behind. Kobalis stayed there with his wife, but one day Sedit
set out on his homeward journey. He talked to all
the birds and animals as he went along, even the
black stumps, for he was glad to be going home. He
shot birds and trapped gophers and went this way for
a time and then he thought he would turn eastward
and visit the Klamath River Indians. Here he fell in
with young crane Torraharsh. All the cranes and other
animals were gambling, playing the straw game, Bo-
hemchooky. Sedit watched them a while and he
thought he must play, too. So he said to the crane,
"Nephew, we will play and win from these fellows.
Your uncle is always lucky; he never loses, or, if he
does, he soon wins it all back again and more with
it."

The crane answered, "How can I play? I have but
little money (beads)." Sedit said, "I will give you
money to play." Many kinds of animals were playing: beavers, foxes, skunks, minks, otters and all
such animals.

So the crane began playing and the first game he lost.
They challenged him to play again. Sedit had been
sitting behind, singing for the crane and betting for
him. So they played again and this time the crane
lost all but one bead. Then they played again and
were lucky and won for a time. But then their luck
changed. They lost and kept losing until they had
lost all they had. Then they bet their hair and lost
it; then their fingernails and lost them; then fingers,

hands, arms, toes, legs, teeth, noses, eyebrows
and lashes. Finally their eyes. All were lost. At
last they bet their hearts and lost them. Everything
had been taken but the hearts and Sedit begged that
they should not be taken until morning.

The other animals agreed to this and that night they
were all in the sweat house where they gambled. Sedit sat alone and whispered to himself and muttered a
charm to make the animals sleep. "Sleep sound so
that we can get away," he said. Soon they were all
asleep and snoring. Then Sedit said to the crane,
"Now, nephew, we must get out of this. This is our
last chance. If they get our hearts we are dead."

So they crept out of the sweat house holding on to
each other, for they were blind and helpless. They
crept along all night and the next day, and for many
days. The sun was hot, for it was summertime, and
at night the mosquitos bit them. They could get
nothing to eat and no water to drink. So they crept
along, always holding hands, until they came out into
Elk Valley, east of Mt. Shasta. Here they sat down
and rested, for it was noontime.

As the crane sat there he heard a noise like water
running, but at first he could not tell if it was only
in his mind or if he really heard water. So he let go
of Sedit, who sat there not knowing anything, and he
felt around and crept in the direction of the sound.
Soon he heard it louder, like a large stream of water
running close by. Soon he could dip his hands in it.
(When Sedit and the crane crawled out of the sweat
house they had regained their form except for their
eyes).

Whenever he dipped in his hands he heard a splash
as of fish getting out of his way. This made him
happy, for he thought if he could catch a fish and
take out its eyes and put them in his empty eye sock-
ets he could regain his sight. So he felt around until
he caught a small trout and took out an eye, but not
being able to see, he put the eye in crooked, and it

was a little crossed.*

Then he could see all around, and it was summer and everything was green. Near him was a bush of serviceberries, so he ate berries for a while and then he went down to the creek and caught another fish and took out an eye and fitted it in his other socket. Then he could see as well as ever and he went back to the berry bush. Some noise he made attracted Sedit's attention from where he sat all doubled up, tired and hungry. "What are you doing? You seem so quiet, nephew. I hear you doing something," he said.

"Uncle, how can I do anything," Torraharsh said, "I sit here, for I am blind."

"But I hear you and it sounds as if you were eating something."

"How can I find anything to eat? I am blind. You are a great magician and have much power. Why do you not get eyes for us? Then we could see to find something to eat."

At last he told Sedit that he was eating serviceberries and gave him some. Sedit thought that he must be able to see. Finally the crane told him how he had put in the fish eyes and was now able to see.

After the crane had told Sedit all this, he went down to the creek and caught two fish and brought them up to him. He took one eye from one of the fish and put it into Sedit's empty socket very carefully.

"Don't be in a hurry, Uncle," said Torraharsh, "I have another eye right here."

So he brought the other eye up carefully in front of Sedit and then slipped it in quickly and Sedit could see as well as ever. He made for the serviceberry bush and began to fill himself with berries. When he had eaten all he could he went down to the creek

---

*Note by E. A. Masson: This is a fact about cranes' eyes.

and tried to drink it dry, he was so thirsty. When
he had enough he said, "Oh, I am glad to be alive!
It is good to be living. Now, nephew, we will travel
down the Sacramento. It is noontime and we will
travel fast and, if we cannot make it, we will stop
and camp."

So they came down east of Mt. Shasta 'til they came
to a place called Kil-charrow-daun (hailstone field)
and Sedit challenged Torraharsh to a footrace. He
said, "Now, nephew, if we should go down below
here and meet someone who would challenge us to a
race, let us try our speed so that we will know. So
if I should run and lose, then you could bet on me to
win. Then Sedit explained to him how they could fool
the other runners and win from them. So they raced
and Sedit was badly handicapped by the deep, soft
sand. But the crane spread his wings and flew over
before Sedit was half way across.

"Wait, nephew," he cried, "wait for me. I cannot
run so fast."

When, at last, he got to the other end, he said,
"Nephew, I am surprised! How can you run so fast?
You can run faster than I can. Now, we will make
a fortune. I have a nephew who can run faster than
I can. We will challenge everybody to foot races.
I will run first and then you will run and win from
everybody."

So they went on down and towards evening they came
to an Indian village. "Now, we will wait until dark,"
Sedit said, "and then we will go in and pretend to be
Fall river Indians, for I can talk any language."

So they waited until dark. "Now," said Sedit, "I will
go first and you come behind me, and I will tell them
that I fell in with you on my way and that we both
have run away from a great Indian uprising, and I will
say to them, 'This poor fellow's relations have all
been captured, and my father and mother and all my
relations have been killed and I have barely escaped,
myself.'" So they went in and Sedit told his story.

"That is very bad. We are very sorry for you," the
people said.

"Yes," said Sedit, "they are coming this way, too.
They may be here by midnight. All you people had
better leave the village and go out and this young
man and myself will keep watch and give the alarm
if they come. But you must give us each a weapon
to defend ourselves with."

So Sedit persuaded all the people to go out into the
woods and told them to listen carefully and he would
give the alarm when he heard the Indians come. As
soon as they had all gone, "Now, nephew," he said,
"let us go quick. This is our chance."

So they took the bows and quivers the people had lent
them and sneaked off silently and hurried away. They
crossed Chow-pui-ken (Huckleberry Valley) and came
down a ridge to Chow-pom-pui-wakit (Soda Creek).
When they came to the mouth of the creek Sedit said,
"Nephew, this is my home now. I will stay here and
you may go on down to your own country. But we will
see each other again sometime and travel together."

"All right," said the crane, and he told the coyote
goodby and rose into the air and flew away down the
river, talking his own language as he flew, after the
manner of cranes. Sedit stood and listened far as he
could hear him down the river, and then went to his
place which was enchanted and was called Khet-ti-
ken-hennis (meaning bitter weeds).*

----

*Note by E. A. Masson: This place is near the former site of Wash
Bailey's hotel at Castle Crags and used to be frequented by the old
Indians for luck in gambling. The spring there is peculiar: a great
number of pine cones wash out from it constantly.

Norwanchakas and His Brother Keriha
Traveling Upward

Norwanchakas and his brother Keriha lived at Naw-
dalt-herril (French Gulch), which means a place of
ruins, or an uninhabited place. Norwanchakas was
the elder brother. Keriha was young and full of tricks
and all kinds of mischief.

One day Norwanchakas said to Keriha, "Brother, let
us travel up to the north and see something of the
world. We do not wish to stay in one place and grow
old here. Let us go and see something."

"All right, let us go," said Keriha. He made his preparation so quickly that he was ready while his brother
was just beginning. These two brothers were giants
and fine, handsome young men.

Norwanchakas took much time and care with his preparation; he wound his hair high in a knot on his head
like the ancient Indian custom, and dressed it with
su-mo-gehas (eagle feathers) and ladil and kotchet
(two kinds of hawk feathers), while Keriha wrapped
his hair in twists each side of his head, hanging down
by his ears, and put in one feather on top, of the bird
called wok-ok. Also, they put on many beads, mem-
pah and moccasins, fine buckskins, armlets of feathers and many ornaments. Norwanchakas used fine
eagle feathers but Keriha had all kinds of common
birds' feathers on his dress.

So they set forth, and named all the creeks and places
of interest as they went along. When they came to
French Gulch Creek they named it Tla-bal-pom. They
came up the creek and turned to the eastward west of
Backbone Creek and Norwanchakas said, "Hereafter,
this place shall be called Ko-pul-su-noh and the
creek is Ko-pul-so-pui-wakit (east creek). So they
traveled on and crossed the ridge Pas-uk-en-koni
(foot of ridge) west of Backbone Creek. Here Norwanchakas told his brother, "Now, this is a dangerous
place; you must be careful and not talk foolishly here

or have any nonsense for you might become exhausted or something happen to us. We are going to travel through here and I shall name all the places for the people who come after and shall foretell what they shall do. But this is a very dangerous place."

He told him all this while they were stopping to rest. Then they came up Backbone Creek and along the ridge. Toward the north and near Dog Creek they named a place Kopas-sow-al-daun (swamp of the cherry tree field) and Norwanchakas said, "These cherry trees shall be here always for the people who come after and will always bear a crop of cherries every summer season."

So they went on and came to a place and called it Thlur-um-puy-uk (hot ashes) and said, "Lubalis, the mountain witches, who can turn themselves to animals or people, as they please, will live here."

From here they came up to Num-da-pompkali (trail to Trinity) and from there to Pu-her-im-ken-yok-as-tun (Lake of the Bleeding Heart). Then Norwanchakas told his brother the story of Wineepoko in times of the long past. "There," said he, pointing to the rocky mountain to the northwest, "is where the Supchet lives."

"Let us go there," said Keriha. And the brother told him no, he must not go there. So they went down the ridge that Wineepoko and his son used to travel until they came to Flume Creek. Near here, opposite where Southern Pacific railroad tunnel number 11 now is, is the hole where the Supchet lives underground and the Indians say it is an underground tunnel running up to Mt. Shasta with a branch running to the mountain where the Supchet had his home when he killed the sons of Wineepoko.

Norwanchakas intended to play a trick upon his brother here for wishing to disobey his orders. He knew that the Supchets had magic powers and sometimes used to come out of their holes and charm people. Norwanchakas had said to his brother when they came down to the ridge, "Stay here and keep a lookout. If you

should see anybody, run and hide or else call me. I
will go on down to the river and spear salmon." And
he went on down 'til he came to the mouth of the tunnel where the Supchet lived and built a big fire there
to smoke out the Supchet.

He took his shield of hardened elk skin and fanned
the smoke into the hole in great clouds. The brother,
watching on the trail, suddenly saw a great cloud of
smoke rise from Mt. Shasta. "What can that be?"
he thought, not knowing that it was from the Supchet's
hole. It puffed out again and again and then one great
cloud, larger than any, rushed out and went floating
and wavering up into the sky and then no more. Norwanchakas had killed the Supchet. He dragged him
out and took off his skin and put it in his quiver and
went to join his brother. "I am out of luck; I speared
no salmon," he said. "Did you see anything?"

"Oh, yes," said Keriha, "I have been calling for you.
I saw a great cloud of smoke puff out of Bohem Puyuik
(Mt. Shasta). I watched it until no more came."

"You are always seeing things," said his brother,
"where I see nothing."

Then they went on down the river 'til they came to
Salmon Falls and Norwanchakas said, "In years to
come many Indians will see this place and see salmon
jumping up here and will know that it is springtime.
I shall call it Deki and the high land above the falls
is Deki-panti."

And they went on down and Norwanchakas named all
the mountains and rocks and creeks and ridges on both
sides of the river.

Norwanchakas was brother to all the small animals:
chu-chu-bakus (chipmunks), chi-hwitl (lizards), tky-
sus (squirrels), dech-lus (ground squirrels) and grass-
hoppers, and they all were glad to see him, for they
knew he would not harm them.

By and by they came to a little ridge called Daw-al
thoul, and then they went on 'til they came to the

mouth of Salt Creek which is called Konuk-pui-dal-
hamis and Norwanchakas said, "In this creek, in the
month of June, the Indians will see many suckers; it
will be full of them, and the Indians will catch them
with nets and spears."

They came to a rock called Che-witl-son, the rock of
the lizard. This rock the present Indians practice
jumping over. Keriha said to his brother, "Look down
there to the eastward, there are people living there."

"Yes," said Norwanchakas, "they are our cousins."
And they went on 'til they came to a little gap called
Wok-kulli. From this little gap they went down, flying very fast to Huy-u-kalli (whistling gap), west of
Southern Pacific railroad tunnel number four. Here
they stopped and Norwanchakas looked over a ridge
and saw the top of a man's head, dressed finely with
feathers which were ornamented with beads and glit-
tered in the sunshine. He came walking slowly up
the river toward Norwanchakas. Norwanchakas knew
that this was his brother who was a great Supchet.
He knew also that they were enemies, and that his
brother, the Supchet, would kill him if possible. So
he said to Keriha, "Let us hurry on down" (meaning,
to get out of the way). But Keriha had already seen
him. "Who is that fine looking fellow?" he said,
"Let me go up to meet him."

"No," said Norwanchakas, "you must stay here and
keep behind me."

So they went on and Norwanchakas and the Supchet
had their bows ready and the arrows on the string and
they threatened one another as they approached. Poor
Keriha stayed behind his brother and peeped out on
each side to see where the Supchet was. At last
they stood face to face, still threatening and muttering
angry words. At last Norwanchakas seized the Supchet and after a hard struggle threw him down and
set his foot on his neck and stamped and kicked him
until he was dead. When he fell his head-knot of
twisted hair and feathers fell off. It can be seen
there to this day in the shape of a large rock, Doli-
el-ked-u-mis (broke against a rock). Also could

be seen the print of the Supchet's breast and knees where he fell, and his footprints where he stood with his feet together, defying Norwanchakas.

When the Supchet had been killed Norwanchakas dragged the body to the river to sink it and he set his foot on it to hold the body down while he piled rocks on it. But whenever he took his foot off, the Supchet's body rose to the top and he could find no rock large enough to hold it down. At last he reached 'way to the westward and got a huge mass of limestone rock from the mountain called Wy-kee-dee-pom (leaning north place) and put it on the Supchet's body. This held him down at last. And the rock can still be seen there in the river, a limestone rock, different from all the other surrounding rocks.

After Norwanchakas and his brother had disposed of the Supchet's body they went on down to the place where the Pit and McCloud rivers join and from there, up the McCloud River until they came to a place between the McCloud and Pit called Nom-dal-ham. Here they found an old man, one of a strange people, catching cheeth (suckers) with a net. He said to them, "Where have you been, my brothers?" Norwanchakas answered that they had been up north a long way but had seen nobody but him.

They talked a long time and Norwanchakas said to the old man, "I am going to Mt. Shasta on the east side to see those people called Bedit. I hear they have many captives and are a terror to all the peoples, far and near." And then he asked him, "Have you seen any warriors around here?"

The old man said he had seen none; so Norwanchakas said that it would be safe for him to go. But Keriha wanted to go to the eastward and follow the Pit River. "That country looks good over there," he said. "Let us go and see the people who live there."

"No," said Norwanchakas, "it is dangerous for us to go to the east; it is a dangerous place. Here, the people speak our language; those over there are fierce warriors and they speak a different language."

They passed the mouth of the McCloud River and Keriha looked across and saw a little smoke wavering up
into the air. "There," he said, "somebody lives
there. Let us go and see them."

"Don't be in a hurry," Norwanchakas said. "We will
see them soon. That is our old aunt who lives there.
She is Kenti-num-op-sik-po-katit. Our brother, Sah-
e-num-cha-bu-too, lives there."

They put their clothes on their head and swam across
the river and went up the trail. As they went, Norwanchakas, after the Indian custom, began telling
who he was and that he had come to see the people
in the house. The old woman heard the voice and was
frightened. She came to the door and peeped out.

"Do not be afraid. It is Norwanchakas and his brother, Keriha. We are your cousins. We have come
to see you and your nephew. We cannot stay long
for we are traveling far, and with a purpose. But I
am glad to see you and our cousin, Sah-e-num-cha-
bu-too." So, still talking, they went in. The nephew had heard the voices and was coming to them as
they talked; yet, he had his bow and arrow ready,
was treachery intended. Norwanchakas and his brother held their arrows ready, too.

Now Sah-e-num-cha-bu-too began telling them that
he had just returned from a great battle where he had
lost a great many warriors, but, at the last, he had
come off victorious, and he thought those people
would trouble him no more.

"I am very glad to hear of your victory," said Norwanchakas, "and now I must go. I have a long journey
yet before me."

"No," said Keriha, let's stay here. This is a good
place." But his brother said, "You must follow me
and go where I go."

So they started out; and Keriha saw so many strange
and new things and different scenery that he went
slowly and Norwanchakas had to wait for him and

hurry him up all the time. When they came to a place,
a big rock, called Wy-to-min, which is called the
sweat house of the tribe Kotchit, or hawks (magic),
Keriha saw numbers of birds flying around the high
rocks, or sitting on them. "Let us go up there and
shoot some of those birds," he said. "I see numbers of them flying all around."

"No," said Norwanchakas, "they are a very bad tribe
and if you went up there they would kill you. It is
a very bad and dangerous place."

At last he got Keriha to go on and leave the hawks but
he still had trouble with the idle one. Did he see salmon in the river, he wanted to spear them and borrowed
a spear from some fishermen on the bank. Or he loiter-
ed among the Indians who were living upon the bank
of the stream. At last Norwanchakas grew tired of
waiting and, since he was now far ahead of his brother, he resolved to frighten him into keeping up with
him. At this time he had just crossed a creek with
high steep banks and was where he could see anyone
coming on the opposite side, so he took the skin of
the dead Supchet out of his quiver and put it on. Then
he waited, lying in the trail. It was forenoon yet.

At last Keriha came in sight on the opposite side of
the creek, hurrying along, for he wished to overtake
his brother. He dropped down the bank, crossed the
creek, and climbed up the steep bank on the other
side. He jumped back with fright! Here was not his
brother but instead a huge monster like nothing he had
ever seen before, and it sprang at him.

"Oh, brother," yelled Keriha, "help! I'm git killed."
And he ran for his life down the steep bank, the animal after him. Poor Keriha ran and ran and the thing
overtook him, passed him and turned as if to spring
upon him. Keriha ran back on the trail with the awful
thing at his heels. Back and forth they ran all day,
Keriha calling in vain for his brother.

Finally Norwanchakas decided his brother had had
enough so he stopped and took off the Supchet's skin
and Keriha saw that it had been his brother who was

the monster. He said, "Oh, why did you frighten me like that? I thought I would be killed!"

"I wish I had frightened you more. Now, maybe, you will try to keep up with me." And he scolded him for his laziness and carelessness.

So they went on again, but Keriha kept close on the heels of Norwanchakas. They traveled up the river 'til they came to the big falls on the McCloud River, Nur-um-wit-ti-dekki (falls where the salmon turn back). Here they met an Indian who asked them where they were going and told them they had come into a very dangerous country. "Do you see that high mountain?" he said, pointing to Mt. Shasta; "Up there on the east side live a people who are very bad. They kill and eat all of us that they capture, and if you do not look out, they will catch you, too. You must be careful and not build a fire."

"No," said Norwanchakas, "we will sleep in the brush."

(Note: The next several pages of Grant's dictation have been lost. We have no account of the action which followed this scene until we find the two men up on Mount Shasta and about to encounter the Bedits.)

At last, about midnight, Norwanchakas and his brother rose up and stole softly to the door of the sweat house. Norwanchakas opened the door quietly and swiftly. On each side of the door a captive was standing, put there to keep watch, by the Bedits, who threatened them with instant death should they fail to give the alarm if an enemy appeared.

Swiftly, Norwanchakas spoke to them, "Don't be afraid and don't make any noise. I have come to save you all!" Then he stole softly around the room and cut the bonds of all the captives. The Bedits lay sleeping around the dying fire which was in the center. Now it flashed up and now it died down, and Norwanchakas went around the room again. This time he tied together the long hair of the sleeping Bedits,

each man tied to the hair of his neighbor. Then he
told the captive guards to come out and go down the
mountain toward the eastward, Keriha being on the
southwest side.

Then he went to Keriha and told him to bring great
quantities of pitch wood and all kinds of wood. So
Keriha did as he was told; then they piled it up all
around the sides of the sweat house and some inside
it. When they had piled it sufficiently high the two
brothers climbed to the roof and sat face to face, one
on each side of the smoke hole in the roof. But they
had first set fire to the wood at the door. Soon the
fire blazed and spread all around and began to burn
the garments of the sleeping Bedits. One woke and
cried, "Something is burning me!" He tried to rise
but found that he was held down by his hair. "Let me
go," he cried. "Why are you pulling my hair?"

"I am not pulling your hair! But you are pulling mine!"
his neighbor cried.

By this time they were all awake, each one crying
out that someone was pulling his hair, and they were
all struggling to get free, the smoke and flames,
meanwhile, getting thicker and hotter. The door was
all red fire and no one could get out. The Bedits
began to fight each other and use their knives and a
terrible battle went on. Many of the Bedits were killed by their companions and many were dying in the
fire.

Norwanchakas and his brother sat watching each side
of the smoke hole and as the souls of the Bedits began
to fly out the smoke hole as red sparks the brothers
struck each one down as it appeared, for they knew
the souls of the Bedits would fly far away and take
shape again if they escaped from the burning sweat
house. As they came thicker and faster Norwanchakas and Keriha had great trouble to strike them all
down. At last there was a mighty rush of smoke and
sparks. They beat them down, all but one which
slipped through the fingers of Norwanchakas and went
soaring up, up to the very top of Bohem Puyuik (Mt.
Shasta). Then the sweat house fell, a heap of ashes,

and the Bedits were dead, all but one, and Norwan-
chakas had seen where it rested. He said to Keriha,
"Let us chase this one and kill him there on Bohem
Puyuik."

So they climbed the high snow peak, and when they
reached the top there was a deep cleft in the rock and
Norwanchakas looked down and someone stretched
hands to him, saying, "Save me!" But Norwanchakas answered, "I will close you in forever!" And
with his two hands he closed the walls of the cleft
together.

There was an end! But if you do not believe this, go
to the top of Bohem Puyuik and listen; deep down in
the rocks you may still hear the imprisoned Bedit
struggling to get free. And the eastern side of Bohem
Puyuik is still blackened from the pitch smoke of the
burning sweat house.

Now Norwanchakas and Keriha flew swift as lightning
back to their own home.

I finish.

A Love Story

Once there lived a young man with his parents at a
place called Tobos-ti (stumpy place) near what is now
called Smithson. He was a great hunter and fisherman
and speared many salmon.

At a place called Tlul-ton (place of ponds) near the
mouth of Salt Creek lived a young girl with her parents, about three miles from Tobos-ti. When this
young man was growing up he used to visit the girl's
home and had made up his mind that he would marry
her when she grew up. But since he had grown older he had not visited her home for some time; yet he
went down past there often with his net and spear to
the falls, Pui-uki-dekki, from where he returned lad-
en with salmon and suckers, as much as he could
carry.

Sometimes he went hunting over at Trinity. Sometimes
he went hunting east to McCloud River.

The young man's father was a very famous hunter, and
because of his skill and wisdom in all manner of hunting he was chosen by the Indians to be the one to call
them all together for the bear drives, deer hunts,
sucker drives or salmon spearing. It was his custom
to send his son to announce to the Indians at such
times that they should congregate. And he taught his
son all his own hunting craft, the best methods to
use, and how to do all things right. "For," said he,
"I grow old, and when I die, you must take up my
skill and do all things right as I have taught you, and
as my father taught me before you."

So one day in the springtime the father told the young
man to go out and tell all the Indians to gather together
for a deer hunt.

The young man went over to Trinity, and then to the
McCloud River, and to Stillwater, and up the Sacramento, and all around where the Indians were. He
was gone three or four days. At last he came back
from his trip, a little tired and weary, and told his
father that they had promised to come.

"That is good," said the father. "It is good to meet
your friends and not live alone in the forest all the
time." So about the third day after the young man
had come home the Indians began arriving, those nearer coming about noon, and it was midnight before the
last ones arrived.

Very early the next morning, long before daylight, the
women were busy making the breakfast for those who
had come to take part in the hunt: great baskets of
acorn mush mixed with dyce (dried salmon) rubbed as
fine as meal, su-muh-bat (sugar pine nuts), boiled
dry salmon and roasted salmon and naup-chu-es
(jerked venison). Also manzanita cider which they
sucked by dipping dried deer tails (chu-ook-us) in
it and drawing the wet brush through the mouth. The
women made all this ready in the sweat house and
some was carried in from the fires outside.

When all was ready the old man mounted the top of the sweat house and made a long speech. He spoke of great hunts and battles in former times, and of hunts and battles which were to come, and talked long of many things. He told them to test their bows before the hunt, pull the strings and see that their flint arrow heads were firmly fastened.

Those who felt too tired for the hunt that day were told they could rest and go the next morning. Finally he told them that he had grown too old to lead them to the hunt himself but that his son should be their leader, as he had trained him in all his knowledge . "Now," he said, "go take your baths and eat so you may hunt with strength and success."

So they all went down to the river and plunged in to refresh themselves and when they came out each one prayed for health and strength, which is the Indian custom. Then they put on their ul-kerris (a red paint which is grease mixed with a red powder), smeared their faces with it and striped their bodies. The Indian doctors put around their necks their woodpecker feathers tipped with rattlesnake rattles. They took their pipes and Indian tobacco and all set out, the young man leading the way.

When they came to a little creek up which they were to go the young man sent a group of five up one side of the creek and another group up the other side, telling them to go ahead of the main body and set snares for the deer.

These snares were made of the twisted fiber of a plant the Wintu Indian calls bok and were very strong. Each man had about ten traps which were made of a short length of rope, about one foot, with a noose on each end, and fastened among the bushes so that the deer would entangle themselves.

These traps were set in a long line or a semicircle and sometimes extended for half a mile. Each man was concealed in the brush a short distance from his own traps so that he might capture and kill the deer that were caught.

After enough time had been allowed to set the traps,
the rest of the Indians began to drive the deer and
other animals up the creek, forming a line on both
sides and closing in from the rear so as to keep the
game in the ravine. The deer, being swift of foot,
went first and many were caught in the snares or killed with arrows. The bears came next, growling and
tearing up the brush, rolling and wallowing along,
uttering wheezing snorts before they were killed.

After the Indians had caught as many deer and bear
as they could they packed them upon their backs and
went home to where the old man awaited them, and
had a great feast for many days. Then they repeated
the hunt and feasted again, keeping this up for a long
time. Finally they broke up camp and returned to their
homes.

The young girl and her parents returned to their home
down the river and the young man and his parents
stayed at their own home and life went on very quietly
for a time.

At last this young girl had grown to be a young woman
and it was time for the Bath-lus-cho-mis (dance of
womanhood). The young man and his parents attended
the dance and the young man fell in love with the girl.
He went home and thought much about her.

In the fall when the salmon were running was the
second, or wind-up, dance for the girl, Kah-chu-nah.
All those who were invited came. When they were
near the place of the dance they put on their ornaments, and the men put on their warrior dress. As
they came near they called aloud to let the people
know they were near. So the old man came out to
meet his friends, telling them of the ones who had
already come from the east, and who were good at
the hweeli (the game of shooting at the pe-lih, a
bundle of sticks or branches about the size of a man
and bound together, and which they shot at from a
distance of 25 or 30 yards). So then the warriors
came running in single file and circling around the
pe-lih.

When they had circled twice around the figure, they stopped and began shooting their arrows into it. The young man was sitting down, watching the performers, not knowing that among them was a young Indian who was to become the girl's lover.

Next they all began to dance the Sedit-chonnus (coyote dance), and in the evening they danced the Round dance. These dances were kept up for three days, at the end of which all returned to their own homes. The young hunter also departed, not knowing that he had a rival.

About three weeks after this the girl's parents left their home and went over to Trinity where they intended to marry the girl to the son of the chief who was living there. The young hunter's father was the first to hear of this and he was sorry for his son, for he knew of his love for the girl.

One morning, soon after this, the young man slept late and his father came and woke him up, saying, "Why do you sleep so late? There must be something wrong. The girl whom you wished to marry, another one has taken her. But people like us are not noticed much; we are not cared for."

The young man said nothing but took his bow and arrows and went to hunt, but for the first time in his life, he killed nothing.

So the months passed and the winter came and went and the young man hoped to hear in the spring that his rival might be dead. Then, one day while out hunting, the young man looked and saw the smoke of fires on the Trinity trail away beyond Sugarloaf Mountain. He went home and told his father what he had seen and the old man said, "How many fires did you see?"

"I saw several at different points on the trail."

"Then someone must be dead," answered the old man, "and they are bringing the body home from Trinity."

The young man wondered much about it. Who could
be dead? Perhaps it might be the girl's husband!

Late that night some Indians came and told them that
the girl was dead and that they were bringing her body
home!

So next day the young man went out to the place where
he had seen the smoke and sang a song of mourning.
He named all the places where he had seen the fires
and came home. He sang "Long time ago you went
west to get the choicest bear hide. Now you come!
Now you come! On the Beaver mountain I see a fire!
I see a fire!"

I finish.

The Lake of the Bleeding Heart

Out west from Castle lake, 'most over to Trinity,
little bit south of Lubalis mountain, there's one lake,
not very big lake. My father he tell me not many
Indians like go there when he young man. He say
his grandfather tell him this story all how that lake
called Bleeding Heart Lake.

Once, oh, long, long time ago, one spirit chief live
by that lake with his one daughter. His old wife she
dead and he raise his little girl baby himself. She
look very nice; nice face and very good her father.
She make many nice cooking baskets. Sometimes she
look 'way over lake, see campfire smoke. She ask
father why no Indians come that lake catchum fish
never no time. He talk spirit talk. He say, "You
big spirit chief girl. That other Indians too bum.
Can't go close to you."

One other spirit chief he live 'way off by Yolla Bolla
Mountain. He young man, grizzly bear man. Well,
he go by sweat house some night, hear Indians talk
in sweat house. One Indian he say he go very close
that lake one time, he see that chief daughter; she
wade out in lake catchum fish. He watch little while.

Girl look towards him. She run out on bank. She turn
to big rock look like shape of heart. Indian man he
scared awful. Run away. Never go back that lake.

That young spirit chief he think, "Can't scare me! I
go that place now; see that spirit girl."

He go that place very quick; not walk, not run. Just
go there all one minute. Those times all big spirit
chiefs he do that way.

When he get there he look very big, very fine. Put
on lots beads, otter skin arrow bag, wear white chief
bone in nose.

Old chief he say, What you do here? You go back
very quick. You poor man. Go very quick or I change
you to rock. I cut your heart out, throw him in lake!"

Young chief he talk old man but he look at girl all
time. She keep head down, work on basket very fast.

Young chief he say he bring old man grizzly bear meat,
he like stay with him. He help him kill deer, catchum
fish, trap otter, trap fishes, trap mink. He make one
spirit sign to old chief. Old chief he say you stay
here. By'm'by I go up to that place. You have my
girl be your wife. Young chief he say you bet you.
Old man talk very nice but he fix to kill young man
that night.

Young man he know by his spirit what old man think,
so when he go lie down to sleep his spirit go 'way
off, talk to girl spirit. She say, "Go look at lake of
water. If look clear then all right, I marry you." And
she walk down by lake on the sandy shore.

Young man he hurry down there. He run fast. He not
see old chief come behind with big bow and spirit arrows. He look on water, moon shine bright on lake.
He see water all red like blood. Girl holler, she say,
"Turn 'round! Turn 'round! Turn 'round!"

Then big spirit chief fight on shore of lake. Girl cry
her father not kill her lover. Old man he say, "I fix

you!" He make her into big rock like heart. She there on shore of lake now. One time I see these things myself in springtime.

Well, sir, they fight all night, all day, next day, Old chief he killum young man, tear out his heart. He take that heart, he put blood all on that big rock that was his girl. He say, "Stand here always and watch. Every spring this time you see the blood come back." Then he throw the heart 'way out in the lake. Big waves come up, he hear big thunder, see big lightning, hearum the young man spirit holler 'way off; sound very sad.

Once more he hear spirit 'way far off. Spirit say gone home to Yolla Bolla; pretty soon to die.

Old chief he go in sweat house. He lie down. Pretty soon he sleep. He fall on hot stones, burn his magic all off. Pretty soon he die.

My father say once he go by that lake, hunt rabbits in springtime. One old Indian go with him. They come down to the lake, see girl. They see the big red rock look like heart. They look on the water, all red like blood. They go 'way quick! Camp other side of range.

All night they hear little owl holler, holler all night. That no good place. They go home. Never see no rabbits.

I finish.